CHANGING SOCIOCULTURAL DYNAMICS AND IMPLICATIONS FOR NATIONAL SECURITY

PROCEEDINGS OF A WORKSHOP

Holly G. Rhodes, *Rapporteur*

Board on Behavioral, Cognitive, and Sensory Sciences

Division of Behavioral and Social Sciences and Education

The National Academies of
SCIENCES · ENGINEERING · MEDICINE

THE NATIONAL ACADEMIES PRESS
Washington, DC
www.nap.edu

THE NATIONAL ACADEMIES PRESS 500 Fifth Street, NW Washington, DC 20001

This activity was supported between the National Academy of Sciences and The Office of the Director of National Intelligence, Contract No. 10003166. Any opinions, findings, conclusions, or recommendations expressed in this publication do not necessarily reflect the views of any organization or agency that provided support for the project.

International Standard Book Number-13: 978-0-309-47377-4
International Standard Book Number-10: 0-309-47377-2
Digital Object Identifier: https://doi.org/10.17226/25056

Additional copies of this publication are available for sale from the National Academies Press, 500 Fifth Street, NW, Keck 360, Washington, DC 20001; (800) 624-6242 or (202) 334-3313; http://www.nap.edu.

Copyright 2018 by the National Academy of Sciences. All rights reserved.

Printed in the United States of America

Suggested citation: National Academies of Sciences, Engineering, and Medicine. (2018). *Changing Sociocultural Dynamics and Implications for National Security: Proceedings of a Workshop*. Washington, DC: The National Academies Press. doi: https://doi.org/10.17226/25056.

The National Academies of
SCIENCES • ENGINEERING • MEDICINE

The **National Academy of Sciences** was established in 1863 by an Act of Congress, signed by President Lincoln, as a private, nongovernmental institution to advise the nation on issues related to science and technology. Members are elected by their peers for outstanding contributions to research. Dr. Marcia McNutt is president.

The **National Academy of Engineering** was established in 1964 under the charter of the National Academy of Sciences to bring the practices of engineering to advising the nation. Members are elected by their peers for extraordinary contributions to engineering. Dr. C. D. Mote, Jr., is president.

The **National Academy of Medicine** (formerly the Institute of Medicine) was established in 1970 under the charter of the National Academy of Sciences to advise the nation on medical and health issues. Members are elected by their peers for distinguished contributions to medicine and health. Dr. Victor J. Dzau is president.

The three Academies work together as the **National Academies of Sciences, Engineering, and Medicine** to provide independent, objective analysis and advice to the nation and conduct other activities to solve complex problems and inform public policy decisions. The National Academies also encourage education and research, recognize outstanding contributions to knowledge, and increase public understanding in matters of science, engineering, and medicine.

Learn more about the National Academies of Sciences, Engineering, and Medicine at **www.nationalacademies.org**.

The National Academies of
SCIENCES • ENGINEERING • MEDICINE

Consensus Study Reports published by the National Academies of Sciences, Engineering, and Medicine document the evidence-based consensus on the study's statement of task by an authoring committee of experts. Reports typically include findings, conclusions, and recommendations based on information gathered by the committee and the committee's deliberations. Each report has been subjected to a rigorous and independent peer-review process and it represents the position of the National Academies on the statement of task.

Proceedings published by the National Academies of Sciences, Engineering, and Medicine chronicle the presentations and discussions at a workshop, symposium, or other event convened by the National Academies. The statements and opinions contained in proceedings are those of the participants and are not endorsed by other participants, the planning committee, or the National Academies.

For information about other products and activities of the National Academies, please visit www.nationalacademies.org/about/whatwedo.

STEERING COMMITTEE ON CHANGING SOCIOCULTURAL DYNAMICS AND IMPLICATIONS FOR NATIONAL SECURITY: A WORKSHOP

JEFFREY JOHNSON (*Chair*), Department of Anthropology, University of Florida
KATHLEEN M. CARLEY, School of Computer Science, Institute for Software Research International, Carnegie Mellon University
MARK LIBERMAN, Department of Linguistics, University of Pennsylvania
DAVID MATSUMOTO, Department of Psychology, College of Science and Engineering, San Francisco State University
JOY ROHDE, Gerald R. Ford School of Public Policy, University of Michigan
SUSAN WELLER, Department of Preventive Medicine and Community Health, The University of Texas Medical Branch

SUJEETA BHATT, *Study Director*
RENÉE WILSON GAINES, *Senior Program Assistant*

COMMITTEE ON A DECADAL SURVEY OF SOCIAL AND BEHAVIORAL SCIENCES FOR APPLICATIONS TO NATIONAL SECURITY

PAUL R. SACKETT (*Chair*), Department of Psychology, University of Minnesota
GARY G. BERNTSON, Department of Psychology, The Ohio State University
KATHLEEN M. CARLEY, School of Computer Science, Institute for Software Research International, Carnegie Mellon University
NOSHIR S. CONTRACTOR, McCormick School of Engineering and Applied Science, School of Communications, and the Kellogg School of Management, Northwestern University
NANCY J. COOKE, The Polytechnic School, Fulton Schools of Engineering, Arizona State University
BARBARA ANNE DOSHER, Department of Cognitive Science, University of California, Irvine
JEFFREY C. JOHNSON, Department of Anthropology, University of Florida
SALLIE KELLER, Biocomplexity Institute, Virginia Polytechnic Institute and State University, National Capital Region
DAVID MATSUMOTO, Department of Psychology, College of Science and Engineering, San Francisco State University
CARMEN MEDINA, MedinAnalytics, LLC
FRAN P. MOORE, CENTRA Technology, Inc.
JONATHAN D. MORENO, Perelman School of Medicine, Department of Medical Ethics and Health Policy, University of Pennsylvania
JOY ROHDE, Gerald R. Ford School of Public Policy, University of Michigan
JEFFREY W. TALIAFERRO, Department of Political Science, Tufts University
GREGORY F. TREVERTON, Dornsife College of Letters, Arts, and Sciences, School of International Relations, University of Southern California
JEREMY M. WOLFE, Brigham and Women's Hospital, Departments of Ophthalmology and Radiology, Harvard Medical School

SUJEETA BHATT, *Study Director*
ALEXANDRA BEATTY, *Senior Program Officer*
JULIE ANNE SCHUCK, *Program Officer*
ELIZABETH TOWNSEND, *Research Associate*
RENÉE L. WILSON GAINES, *Senior Program Assistant*

BOARD ON BEHAVIORAL, COGNITIVE, AND SENSORY SCIENCES

SUSAN T. FISKE (*Chair*), Department of Psychology and Woodrow Wilson School of Public and International Affairs, Princeton University
JOHN BAUGH, Department of Arts & Sciences, Washington University in St. Louis
LAURA L. CARSTENSEN, Department of Psychology, Stanford University
JUDY DUBNO, Department of Otolaryngology-Head and Neck Surgery, Medical University of South Carolina
JENNIFER EBERHARDT, Department of Psychology, Stanford University
ROBERT L. GOLDSTONE, Department of Psychological and Brain Sciences, Indiana University
DANIEL R. ILGEN, Department of Psychology, Michigan State University
JAMES S. JACKSON, Institute for Social Research, University of Michigan
NANCY G. KANWISHER, Department of Brain and Cognitive Sciences, Massachusetts Institute of Technology
JANICE KIECOLT-GLASER, Department of Psychology, The Ohio State University College of Medicine
BILL C. MAURER, School of Social Sciences, University of California, Irvine
JOHN MONAHAN, School of Law, University of Virginia
STEVEN E. PETERSEN, Department of Neurology and Neurological Surgery, Washington University School of Medicine
DANA M. SMALL, Department of Psychiatry, Yale Medical School
TIMOTHY J. STRAUMAN, Department of Psychology and Neuroscience, Duke University
JEREMY M. WOLFE, Brigham and Women's Hospital, Departments of Ophthalmology and Radiology, Harvard Medical School

BARBARA A. WANCHISEN, *Director*
THELMA COX, *Program Coordinator*

Acknowledgments

This Proceedings of a Workshop was reviewed in draft form by individuals chosen for their diverse perspectives and technical expertise. The purpose of this independent review is to provide candid and critical comments that will assist the National Academies of Sciences, Engineering, and Medicine in making each published proceedings as sound as possible and to ensure that it meets the institutional standards for quality, objectivity, evidence, and responsiveness to the charge. The review comments and draft manuscript remain confidential to protect the integrity of the process.

We thank the following individuals for their review of this proceedings: Susan Brandon, Defense Intelligence Agency, and Susan C. Weller, Department of Preventive Medicine and Community Health and Department of Family Medicine, University of Texas Medical Branch, Galveston.

Although the reviewers listed above provided many constructive comments and suggestions, they were not asked to endorse the content of the proceedings, nor did they see the final draft before its release. The review of this proceedings was overseen by John Monahan, School of Law, University of Virginia. He was responsible for making certain that an independent examination of this proceedings was carried out in accordance with standards of the National Academies and that all review comments were carefully considered. Responsibility for the final content rests entirely with the rapporteur and the National Academies.

Jeffrey Johnson, *Chair*
Steering Committee on Changing Sociocultural
Dynamics and Implications for National Security

Contents

1 **INTRODUCTION** 1
  The Decadal Survey of Social and Behavioral Sciences for
    Applications to National Security, 1
  Objectives for the Six Workshops, 3
  Introduction to the Workshop on Changing Sociocultural
    Dynamics and Implications for National Security, 4
  Structure of This Proceedings, 6

2 **LINKING CULTURE, LANGUAGE, BEHAVIOR, AND DATA** 7
  Measuring Individuals: How Cultural Values Shape Public
    Perceptions of Risk, 7
  Examining Shared Beliefs and Behaviors: Living up to Cultural
    Ideals, 11
  Identifying Patterns: Understanding Culture through Social
    Media, 14
  Discussion, 17

3 **TRIANGULATION OF DATA SOURCES AND RESEARCH
    METHODS** 21
  Using Multiple Sources of Data to Understand Conflict in
    Organizations, 21
  Using Data from Surveys, Laboratory Experiments, and Social
    Media to Understand Misinformation, 24
  Challenges in Triangulating Health Care Data, 28
  Discussion, 32

| 4 | **THE CHALLENGE OF MULTIPLE LEVELS OF ANALYSIS** | 37 |

Levels of Influence, 37
Patterns of Cultural Variation, 40
Levels of Analysis and Linguistics, 45
Discussion, 48
Wrap-up, 51

APPENDIXES

A	Statement of Task for the Decadal Survey of Social and Behavioral Sciences for Applications to National Security	53
B	Workshop Agenda	55
C	Participants List	61
D	Biographical Sketches of Steering Committee Members and Presenters	67

1

Introduction

The Office of the Director of National Intelligence (ODNI), which oversees and directs the work of the 17 agencies and organizations responsible for foreign, military, and domestic intelligence for the United States, has interest in research from the social and behavioral sciences that may be beneficial to the Intelligence Community (IC). To develop a systematic understanding of these potential benefits, ODNI requested that the National Academies of Sciences, Engineering, and Medicine conduct a decadal survey of the social and behavioral sciences to identify research opportunities that show promise for supporting national security efforts in the next 10 years.

THE DECADAL SURVEY OF SOCIAL AND BEHAVIORAL SCIENCES FOR APPLICATIONS TO NATIONAL SECURITY

A decadal survey is a method for engaging members of a research community to identify lines of research with the greatest potential utility in the pursuit of a particular goal. The National Academies pioneered this type of survey with a study of ground-based astronomy in 1964.[1] Since then, committees appointed by the National Academies have conducted more than 15 decadal surveys. The Decadal Survey of Social and Behavioral Sciences for Applications to National Security represents the first opportunity to apply this approach to the social and behavioral sciences.

---

[1] National Academy of Sciences. (1964). *Ground-Based Astronomy: A Ten-Year Program.* Washington, DC: National Academy Press. doi: https://doi.org/10.17226/13212.

Its purpose is to develop an understanding of the lines of research in these fields that offer the greatest potential to enhance the capabilities of the IC. To carry out this work, the National Academies appointed the Committee on the Decadal Survey of Social and Behavioral Sciences for Applications to National Security (Decadal Survey Committee); the committee's charge appears in Appendix A.

The Decadal Survey Committee has pursued many avenues in collecting information about the needs of the IC and relevant cutting-edge research in the social and behavioral sciences. As part of its information-gathering process, the committee held a series of six workshops—the first three on October 11, 2017, and the second three on January 24, 2018.[2] These workshops, for which planning began early in the committee process, were designed to explore areas about which the committee wished to learn more and to allow the committee to engage with a broad range of experts. The topics selected for the workshops do not necessarily indicate the ultimate direction of the committee's deliberations. The six topics addressed by the workshops were

1. changing sociocultural dynamics and implications for national security;
2. emerging trends and methods in international security;
3. leveraging advances in social network thinking for national security;
4. learning from the science of cognition and perception for decision making;
5. workforce development and intelligence analysis; and
6. understanding narratives for national security purposes.

Separate steering committees, whose membership included both members of the Decadal Survey Committee and additional experts in the topics to be addressed, were appointed to plan these workshops. Each of these committees was guided by its own charge. All were asked to bring their expertise to bear in identifying specific areas of promising research and experts with deep knowledge who could offer a range of insights.

This Proceedings of a Workshop, prepared by the workshop rapporteur, summarizes the presentations and discussions at the first workshop, on changing sociocultural dynamics and implications for national security.[3] This workshop was planned by the Steering Committee on Changing Sociocultural Dynamics and Implications for National Security, whose charge is

---

[2] For more information about the Decadal Survey and all of the workshops, see http://nas.edu/SBSDecadalSurvey [January 2018].

[3] The archived Webcast of the workshop and available presentations can be found at http://sites.nationalacademies.org/DBASSE/BBCSS/DBASSE_181265 [November 2017].

INTRODUCTION 3

> **BOX 1-1**
> **Workshop Steering Committee Charge**
>
> An ad hoc steering committee will plan and conduct a 1-day public workshop. The workshop will feature invited presentations and discussions to explore the current state of the science regarding culture, language, and behavior for national security contexts. The committee will plan and organize the workshop, select speakers and discussants, and moderate the discussions at the workshop. The workshop will be part of a set of workshops designed to gather information for the Decadal Survey of Social and Behavioral Sciences for Applications to National Security. A Proceedings of the Workshop will be prepared by a designated rapporteur in accordance with institutional guidelines.

presented in Box 1-1. The workshop's purpose was to explore the current state of the science regarding culture, language, and behavior with respect to the national security context. It should be noted that the steering committee's role was limited to planning and convening the workshop, and that the views contained in this proceedings are those of individual workshop participants and do not necessarily represent the views of all workshop participants, the steering committee, or the National Academies. The agenda for the workshop appears in Appendix B; a list of individuals who attended the three workshops held on October 11, 2017, is presented in Appendix C; and biographical sketches of the committee members and speakers are provided in Appendix D.

OBJECTIVES FOR THE SIX WORKSHOPS

In an opening session for the three October 11, 2017, workshops, the chair of the Decadal Survey Committee, Paul Sackett, University of Minnesota, and sponsor representative David Honey, ODNI, provided background information on the objectives for the six workshops.

Sackett noted that the Decadal Survey Committee will rely heavily on input from experts in the communities of national security and behavioral and social science research. Given the breadth of the committee's charge, he explained, it must cast a wide net, extending well beyond the specific expertise of its members. He described the six workshops as an important part of the effort to gather ideas. The workshops would support the committee by helping to identify promising research areas and allowing the committee members to engage in discussion with experts in a wide range of areas salient to its work.[4]

Honey expressed appreciation to all those contributing to the committee's work through the workshops and other activities, noting that the participation of the full range of experts in the intelligence and behavioral and social science communities would be needed to make the decadal study successful. Making predictions about future directions for research is difficult, he acknowledged, but in his view it is necessary. He noted that the final report of the Decadal Survey Committee will be "a very powerful tool" for government officials who must make decisions regarding funding and other priorities. The decadal model, he explained, "offered the best opportunity" to identify research directions and priorities that reflect a wide range of insights and perspectives. "Decision makers are really asking much deeper and more probing questions today than we've seen before," he said. "They really want to know why surprising movements such as the Arab Spring [uprisings that began in 2010] occur. The national security community is eager for new ways to understand such events and how to respond to them, and also for better ways to assess their interventions after the fact." Honey thanked the participants for contributing, emphasizing that their ideas would be "crucial for getting us where we need to go."

INTRODUCTION TO THE WORKSHOP ON CHANGING SOCIOCULTURAL DYNAMICS AND IMPLICATIONS FOR NATIONAL SECURITY

Steering committee chair Jeffrey Johnson, University of Florida, opened the workshop by noting that multiple perspectives are essential for advancing methodology in the study of sociocultural dynamics over the coming decade. To set the stage for discussion of the new research frontiers brought together for this workshop, Joy Rohde, University of Michigan, provided an overview of ethical considerations for digital research in the social and behavioral sciences. She remarked that although new computer technology and the vast amounts of data it can provide offer unprecedented opportunities to measure culture, linguistics, and behavior in new ways, these opportunities also present important ethical challenges. She observed that digital research, which includes "big data," machine learning, new computing tools, and new data sources, can enhance sociocultural analysis in support of national security. In her view, however, the nature of digital technologies also presents specific ethical challenges: "The scale, the speed, the wide

---

[4] Other activities associated with the Decadal Survey include calls for white papers, public meetings, and an online discussion forum; see http://nas.edu/SBSDecadalSurvey [December 2017].

distribution of monitoring and tracking capabilities as well as the ease and the distance with which we can spread data raises new potentials for risk of harms," she explained. Such concerns were also raised in the Menlo report[5] commissioned by the Department of Homeland Security, she added.

One concern is privacy, Rohde noted. Individual research subjects can possibly be identified even when datasets are anonymized, she explained, because data on people's behaviors are available on such a granular level. According to Rohde, ethicists increasingly agree that traditional norms and protections for human subjects in social and behavioral science research are insufficient for digital research. Traditional privacy protections have focused on protecting personal identifying or sensitive information. However, Rohde explained, people's expectations and concerns about their control of records of their personal behavior that are now available vary by context and culture. To illustrate this point, she contrasted expectations of privacy on Twitter and expectations of the privacy of one's cell phone records or e-mail. Paraphrasing Helen Nissenbaum of New York University, she explained that privacy is the right neither to secrecy nor to control, but rather the right to determine the appropriate flow of personal information.

Digital research also poses special concern with regard to fairness and justice, stated Rohde, because of an imbalance of power in the control of information. She observed that there is a high cost to opting out of using digital services, such as e-mail, so users perceive that they have little choice but to accede to service agreements. Accordingly, she said, service agreements are inconsistent with the premises of traditional informed consent, in which high stakes for nonparticipation are considered unethical. She added that users typically know that information about them is gathered if they use digital services, but they often do not know how this information is used.

Rohde argued that it is important for social and behavioral science researchers to consider these ethical issues because the judgments they reach and the way they categorize behavior can have a material effect on people's lives and well-being. Therefore, she asserted, researchers have an obligation to use methods that are verifiable and sound. Beyond these concerns, she added, are particular concerns with conducting social and behavioral science research in the context of national security. The public is concerned about surveillance, she noted, and failure to take these concerns seriously can have a chilling effect on research and erode public trust both in research and in the IC. She urged workshop participants to "think about all the

---

[5]Dittrich, D., and Kenneally, E. (2012). *The Menlo Report: Ethical Principles Guiding Information and Communication Technology Research*. Technical Report. Washington, DC: U.S. Department of Homeland Security.

possibilities of big data and how we can design and carry out social and behavioral science research in ways that address these ethical concerns."

STRUCTURE OF THIS PROCEEDINGS

This proceedings follows the structure of the workshop. Chapter 2 summarizes the presentations and discussion in the first workshop panel, which addressed how research using big data can shed light on culture, language, and behavior, with a focus on links between recent developments in the quantitative measurement of culture and the work of experts in social computing and computational social science.[6] The presentations and discussion summarized in Chapter 3 examined strategies for linking different types of research that can contribute to understanding these phenomena, bringing several perspectives to two challenges for cultural, linguistic, and behavioral research: multiple-method (or triangulation) and multiple-site (replication) research designs. In his introductory remarks, Johnson noted that these two approaches are increasingly being used across the behavioral and social sciences and hold potential for meaningful progress in distinguishing features that are unique to individual cultures from those that are universal. Finally, Chapter 4 turns to the presentations and discussion on the challenge of working across multiple levels of analysis. In describing this panel, Johnson observed that social and behavioral science researchers may focus on individuals or social groups from small units up to the level of societies, and that working at different levels requires different types of analyses and tools. He added that working in the national security context, in which traditional fieldwork is rarely practical, poses an additional challenge.

---

[6] "Computational social science" refers to the academic subdisciplines concerned with computational approaches to the social sciences, which means that computers are used to model, simulate, and analyze social phenomena. Social computing is an area of computer science that is concerned with the intersection of social behavior and computational systems. It is based on creating or re-creating social conventions and social contexts through the use of software and technology.

2

Linking Culture, Language, Behavior, and Data

Panel moderator Susan Weller, University of Texas Medical Branch, introduced the first workshop panel by explaining that three different approaches to studying culture, language, and behavior emerge from social psychology, anthropology, and digital research and network analysis:

1. using a series of related questions about attitudes, beliefs, perceptions, etc., to identify individual differences and create typologies of people within a culture;
2. using a series of related questions to estimate a group's best response to each question, which allows for the examination of shared beliefs and behaviors as a way of identifying what is normative in a culture, a model that has proven adaptable to multiple forms of data and statistical approaches; and
3. using naturally occurring or observed language, responses, and images to identify patterns and clusters of behavior at both the individual and group levels.

Presentations in this session illustrated how each of these approaches provides a unique way of understanding culture.

MEASURING INDIVIDUALS: HOW CULTURAL VALUES SHAPE PUBLIC PERCEPTIONS OF RISK

Dan Kahan, Yale University, presented his work on how beliefs and values can influence perceptions of science communication and the way people process information about risk. Under a simple Bayesian model, he observed, individuals would revise an existing belief in proportion to how much more or less consistent it was with new evidence relative to some alternative belief. However, he explained, people do not think this way. Instead, he said, people are subject to confirmation bias, a phenomenon in which they assign weight to new evidence based on its consistency with what they already believe. He noted that this tendency limits the likelihood or speed with which people will revise mistaken beliefs.

Kahan and his colleagues have tested a model that helps explain how this bias may occur in the first place. According to this cultural cognition model, Kahan explained, people use their cultural worldviews—preferences about how society should be organized—to motivate their search for and processing of information. He added that people search for new information that is consistent with the positions of their affinity groups; in addition, "no matter where the information comes from, they are going to selectively credit it and discredit it in patterns that reflect and reinforce the position on some disputed policy fact within their group, and usually contrary to some competing group." Because people repeatedly apply this strategy, he continued, they develop a set of prior beliefs about an issue, and confirmation bias comes into play because those prior beliefs are highly correlated with the way they select and process new information. However, he said, a third variable—cultural worldview—determines both prior beliefs and information seeking and processing.

Kahan presented evidence that supports this model. He cited one study that examined the views about nanotechnology of a nationally representative sample of 1,850 people.[1] He and his colleagues gathered survey data on participants' worldviews to determine where they fell on a spectrum from individualism to communitarianism (the survey questions assessed the degree to which participants felt that individuals should be responsible for their own well-being, without the assistance or interference of the collective). The researchers also measured hierarchical and egalitarian views. Referring to Figure 2-1, Kahan explained that the interaction or combinations of people's views on these dimensions tend to fall in patterns, which can be categorized in four groups that provide a powerful way to predict people's risk perceptions. For example, he said, people who hold more communitarian hierarchical views (i.e., the upper right quadrant of the figure) tend to believe that the collective, represented by officials with rank and authority, should be securing the well-being of all individuals within the collective and overriding individual choices to do so. On the other hand, he noted, people with more egalitarian views believe authorities should not

---

[1] Kahan, D.M., Braman, D., Slovic, P., Gastil, J., and Cohen, G. (2009). Cultural cognition of the risks and benefits of nanotechnology. *Nature Nanotechnology,* 4(2), 87–90.

LINKING CULTURE, LANGUAGE, BEHAVIOR, AND DATA 9

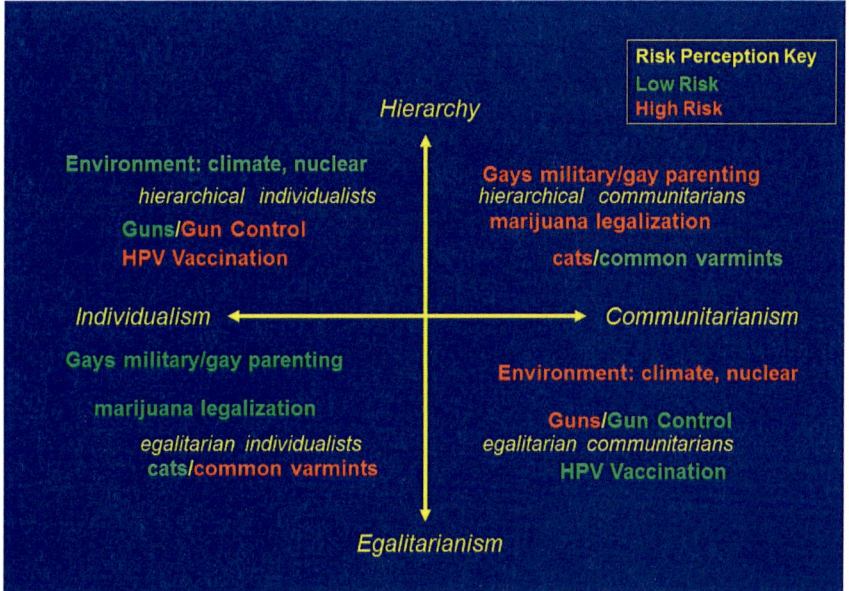

FIGURE 2-1 Cultural cognition worldviews.
SOURCE: Presentation by Dan Kahan at the workshop.

dictate individual choices. With regard to specific risks, he continued, the hierarchical individualist tends to be skeptical about environmental risk, whereas egalitarians and communitarians tend to be very concerned about those same risks.

To explore the impact of people's worldview on their perception of risk, Kahan explained how the four different groups depicted in Figure 2-1 view gun control laws and regulations. Kahan and his colleagues found that those with hierarchical worldviews tend to view a gun as a piece of equipment that both provides its owner with status as a protector or hunter and reduces the risk of violent predation. In contrast, they found that egalitarians and communitarians perceive more risk to owning a gun and associate guns with patriarchy or assassinations of egalitarian leaders.

Kahan reported that the research showed similar patterns in the study participants' views of environmental risk, but the researchers were also interested in participants' reactions to a topic about which they were learning for the first time. To gather this information, participants were surveyed on the subject of nanotechnology. Kahan reported that although about 80 percent of participants had not heard of the technology or did not know how it is used, about 90 percent had an opinion on whether it was safe. Kahan and his colleagues measured participants' perceptions of the risks and benefits of nanotechnology, then assigned the participants to one of two experimental groups: one group received no information about nanotechnology beyond a minimal definition; the other received a single paragraph describing the benefits of nanotechnology and another describing some of its potential risks.

According to Kahan, the results of this experiment showed that about 61 percent of the group that received no information about nanotechnology perceived it as safe. Hierarchical individualists and egalitarian communitarians, who tended to disagree about environmental risk, did not differ significantly in their views about the risks of nanotechnology. However, Kahan reported, participants in the group that received information splintered in ways consistent with the patterns already noted in the views of hierarchical individualists and egalitarian communitarians regarding environmental risk.

In their study, Kahan and his colleagues also investigated the finding from other surveys that the more people know about nanotechnology, as determined by their self-reported familiarity with the technology, the more they like it. Participants in their study showed a similar pattern, Kahan reported: those who were more familiar with nanotechnology indicated more strongly that its benefits would outweigh its risks, whereas the positions of those in the group receiving information diverged, correlating with their cultural outlooks. He added that those who professed to be unafraid of nanotechnology were also less concerned about other potential risks, such as those posed by the Internet, mad cow disease, or private gun ownership. "It is not the case that learning about nanotechnology makes you not worry about other things," he said, "There must be some third variable that is both making people familiar with nanotechnology and not concerned about those things." He concluded that his team's experiment supports the cultural cognition model, which suggests that people's worldviews, rather than their prior beliefs, explain how they process new information about risk.

Kahan's subsequent research has focused on identifying the particular mechanisms that bias the search for and processing of information, including the individual characteristics that accentuate or suppress this processing. Contrary to expectations, he explained, people who displayed the greatest proficiency in understanding scientific evidence (i.e., higher scores on measures of critical thinking, science literacy, or interpretation of quantitative information) were the most polarized on issues. He added that subsequent experiments showed that people use these skills to find and rationalize or dismiss information consistent with the views of their worldview group. When people indicate a high level of curiosity about science or interest in consuming scientific information, he observed, they tend to be less polarized. Some evidence suggests, he noted, that professional judgment can limit the effects of worldview on information processing, but he suggested that this is an area requiring more study.

Kahan closed by suggesting several research questions that might be worthy of future study. With respect to the question of whether professional judgment provides a level of immunity from bias in processing information, he observed, it would be interesting to study professionals who evaluate and make policy related to national security risks. He also pointed to the potential utility of research on how institutional cultures create affinity groups that affect how people process information. "The affinity groups could be anything," he elaborated. "They are ones that are important to people's status because people will judge you based on holding beliefs that are characteristic of the group, and they become almost badges of identity and loyalty." He suggested further that future research could perhaps examine the effects of group identity among people drawn to terrorism. He remarked that such questions could be explored through collaborations between researchers and professionals who work in national security settings.

EXAMINING SHARED BELIEFS AND BEHAVIORS: LIVING UP TO CULTURAL IDEALS

William Dressler, University of Alabama, described advances made in studying "cultural consonance," which involves modeling the degree to which individuals' own beliefs and behaviors are similar to the prototypes for belief and behavior encoded in the shared ideas and practices of a culture. He explained that the concept of cultural consonance is embedded in a larger body of theory about what culture is and how it affects groups and individuals. While an examination of this complex body of work was beyond the scope of the workshop, he noted that cultural knowledge is a property of a social group but is also possessed by each of the individuals in that group. Viewing cultural knowledge this way, he added, allows researchers to describe intracultural diversity; the differences between culture and individual beliefs and attitudes; and the relationships among human culture, behavior, and biology.

The cultural consensus model[2] played a key role in advancing the study of culture, Dressler continued, because it provided a model for observing and measuring the knowledge that is shared and how it is distributed among individuals. He explained that research based on this model involved first testing the overall consensus among individuals regarding their knowledge of a cultural domain (e.g., family life), and then calculating an

---

[2] Romney, A.K., Weller, S.C., and Batchelder, W.H. (1986). Culture as consensus: A theory of culture and informant accuracy. *American Anthropologist, 88*(2), 313–338.

individual's degree of cultural knowledge based on this "cultural answer key" (i.e., consensus). He added that this model can also be useful for identifying culturally contested models or subcultures.

Dressler said he employs a two-stage process to study how people incorporate cultural knowledge into their own beliefs and behaviors. He first explores the cultural domains of interest to identify the content and structure of cultural models and to determine the degree to which these are shared among individuals. Second, he collects extensive survey data on the extent to which individuals hold this cultural knowledge (cultural consonance) and its association with health outcomes. Dressler described research he has conducted in Brazil to illustrate this approach.[3]

Dressler and his colleagues began by identifying cultural domains that were significant for people's everyday lives in the Brazilian city of Ribeirão Preto: lifestyle, social support, family life, national identity, and occupational and educational aspirations. These domains, he explained, either arose in spontaneous conversations with people or were of specific theoretical interest in the study of health and disease. Dressler asked study participants to list words they associated with each cultural domain. For family life, for example, participants generated a list of terms they associated with a prototypically "good" Brazilian family (e.g., "love" and "religious"). To assess lifestyle, the researchers asked participants to describe valued material goods and leisure time activities (e.g., a house of one's own or going to the movies) and to rank the terms that were generated by importance. The terms were also sorted by additional characteristics, such as whether they were positive or negative with respect to family life.

Dressler explained that the next step was to conduct a cultural consensus analysis, which involved asking respondents to rate the importance of each term associated with family life and lifestyle and then analyzing the correlations among the responses. These data were then used to create measures against which individual responses were compared. In the case of the lifestyle domain, Dressler and his colleagues developed a checklist of the terms identified as most important and used it to create a survey of family life that measured the respondents' perceptions of their own families relative to each of those terms.

According to Dressler, "With this measurement model, we can draw a straight line connecting the spontaneous speech of Brazilians to a measure that orders individuals along a continuum derived from the way they themselves talk about the domain." He explained that this measurement approach provides a high level of validity from the perspective of those

---

[3] Dressler, W.W., Balieiro, M.C., and dos Santos, J.E. (2017). Cultural consonance in life goals and depressive symptoms in urban Brazil. *Journal of Anthropological Research*, 73(1), 43–65.

within the culture being studied and can be adapted to virtually any domain of interest.

Dressler continued by observing that even if there is a high degree of agreement about ideals within important domains in a culture, not everyone achieves these ideals. He and his colleagues developed an additional survey to examine the relationship of this "cultural consonance" to health outcomes, such as blood pressure and depression, at multiple points in time. They found that survey respondents who showed the lowest consonance with cultural ideals related to social support tended to have higher systolic blood pressure, a finding replicated after a period of 10 years.

Dressler added that consonance with family life ideals was also associated with a lower incidence of depression, a relationship even more pronounced for people from low-income neighborhoods. According to Dressler, this research shows that cultural consonance with ideals of family life plays a role in how the genetic predisposition for depression and its interaction with childhood adversity manifest in symptoms of depression. He added that in a 2-year longitudinal study he and his colleagues found that changes in cultural consonance were associated with changes in depressive symptoms. More recently, he and his team have found that cultural consonance in life goals mediates depressive symptoms relative to both socioeconomic status and a sense of one's own personal agency.[4,5] Moreover, he reported, other researchers have linked cultural consonance with other health outcomes, such as body composition, stress in pregnancy, and Internet gaming addiction.[6] Research of this kind has pointed to the significant role of cultural domains in many cultures around the globe, he noted.

Dressler concluded by suggesting how this methodology could be used with more extensive forms of data collection. In his view, data for the second phase of his approach—measuring individual beliefs and behaviors—could be gathered in a variety of ways and organized in terms of cultural domains and elements derived in the first phase of the process, the cultural modeling phase. "It is through the cultural modeling phase," he elaborated, "that we can locate groups and individuals in a cultural space of their own construction."

---

[4]Dressler, W.W., Balleiro, M.C., Ribeiro, R., and dos Santos, J.E. (2007). A prospective study of cultural consonance and depressive symptoms in urban Brazil. *Social Science & Medicine*, 65(10), 2058–2069.

[5]Dressler, W.W. (2016). *Cultural Consonance, Personal Agency, and Depressive Symptoms in Urban Brazil*. Abstracts of the 2016 Annual Meeting of the Society for Applied Anthropology, March 29–April 3, Vancouver, BC, Canada.

[6]Dressler, W.W. (2018). *Culture and the Individual: Theory and Method of Cultural Consonance*. New York: Routledge.

IDENTIFYING PATTERNS:
UNDERSTANDING CULTURE THROUGH SOCIAL MEDIA

Dhiraj Murthy, University of Texas at Austin, described research in which he and his colleagues have measured aspects of culture using large sets of visual data (big data), as well as explored how information spreads through networks of people. He explained that they have combined this research with what they describe as in-depth contextualized analysis of social media content across a variety of social media platforms, such as Twitter, Facebook, Instagram, Snapchat, and WhatsApp.

Murthy began his description of this research by noting several challenges unique to studying culture through social media. First, he observed, the information available about users is incomplete. But perhaps more significant, he said, is that the data are often visual: textual data are far easier to gather and to code into categories relative to visual data, particularly when researchers are using very large datasets. Murthy explained that he has developed a method for coding large sets of images and videos so they can be grouped in categories, archetypes, or models for analysis, and that this method can be automated so it can be used at the big data level.

Another challenge, Murthy continued, is that algorithms used by such providers as YouTube and Facebook to determine what content people see are proprietary and inaccessible to researchers and others. He characterized this as a particular challenge to studying how media content influences people and spreads through networks. He noted that Twitter has been studied more frequently than other social media platforms in part because its interface facilitates gathering and working with its textual data. While some Twitter research has focused on sentiment analysis,[7] Murthy has pursued ways to code social media information along other dimensions using an open coding model. He explained that closed coding systems (e.g., sorting into predefined categories) are easier to work with than open coding systems (e.g., sorting into categories created based on the information gathered). However, he said, although open coding models are "messy" and difficult, they allow researchers to develop explanations of phenomena that emerge from collected visual data and are not dictated by prior conceptions.

Murthy described his analytic techniques as both abductive and retroductive. He explained that abductive reasoning has been defined as "finding the best explanations among a set of possible ones,[8] whereas retroductive

---

[7] For more on Twitter research, see Zimmer, M., and Proferes, N.J. (2014). A topology of Twitter research: Disciplines, methods, and ethics. *Aslib Journal of Information Management,* 66(3), 250–261.

[8] Abduction is used to determine a logical assumption, explanation, inference, conclusion, hypothesis, or best guess via observation. For more information, see Paul, G. (1993). Approaches to abductive reasoning: An overview. *Artificial Intelligence Review,* 7(2), 109–152.

methods are abductive approaches used to identify reasons and causes for possible explanations.⁹

As described by Murthy, the process for coding visual data is an iterative one that involves coding and repeatedly reexamining new data to test and refine categories and concepts suggested by the data. "What is happening in terms of this YouTube video or in terms of an Instagram image? . . . We cannot understand all the motivations for why someone is posting this type of content because we do not know a lot about them. We are dealing with very sparse data," he noted. To determine how to classify visual information and to understand how information circulates among a network of people, he and his team conduct network analysis, using the hashtags associated with images or videos to understand how information diffuses across a network of people. Although identifying meaningful visual attributes currently requires human coding, he and his team are seeking ways to apply the codes they develop to big data methods or other uses. In addition to examining online content, they examine data associated with the specific social media application.

Murthy described an example of how this methodology has been applied. He explained that he uses YouTube because it is one of the few social media application programming interfaces (APIs) that is very open and allows for active access for weeks at a time, enabling researchers to accumulate large volumes of video data. Social media platforms play an important role in radicalization, he noted, and journalists have reported that the Islamic State in Iraq and Syria (ISIS) uses social media as a key part of its recruiting strategy. Therefore, Murthy and his colleagues sought to better understand the role of videos in radicalization. He added that although Islamic State content is regularly deleted from social media platforms, it is also quickly reposted. He and his team looked specifically at which types of videos include recommendations for additional radical videos, what linguistic or other markers could identify this radical content, and what methods could be used effectively to classify such videos.

Murthy and his team identified 15 video titles mentioned in news articles as officially attributed to ISIS. Of these, they were able to locate and verify 11 as Al Hayat videos (officially produced by ISIS), and they used these 11 videos as "seeds." One example of a seed video was a "Mujatweet." According to Murthy, such often-used videos were designed to be tweet-sized for YouTube and reposted by ISIS YouTube bots whenever they were removed. Other seed videos had a more documentary style, he noted.

Murthy explained that each of these seeds recommended additional videos, which in turn recommended still others, so he and his colleagues

---

⁹For more on retroductive methods, see Olsen, W.K. (2012). *Data Collection: Key Debates and Methods in Social Research*. Thousand Oaks, CA: SAGE.

ultimately identified millions of videos, although this larger pool included both official ISIS videos and completely unrelated content (e.g., videos related to gaming). He and his team selected a sample of these videos, coded them according to their attributes, and developed a framework to explain patterns observed in the videos by coders. Murthy noted that this method is a way to reverse engineer the information being sought. He described the selection of content to be displayed to users in search results or as "recommended" content as a "black box." Because researchers lack access to the proprietary search data used by YouTube and other platforms, he said, "We do not know what percentage of users explicitly search for ISIS content versus [experiencing] 'accidental' exposure."

Murthy added that examining the YouTube API allows him and his colleagues to determine whether a video is recommending additional radical videos, and that this information can be used to create a map of connected videos. In addition, the researchers are able to capture information about whether a user has watched a particular video, although the interface does not provide access to user search terms. The video content recommended to users when they view radical videos is what Murthy uses as an outcome measure: "Even though I cannot see the keywords that people are searching, at least I can approximate in some ways or try to measure some of their experience and also see how the algorithm is behaving in terms of recommendation," he said. The recommended video feature of YouTube, combined with its autoplay of the next recommended video, tends to lead people to watch many videos in a row, a finding confirmed by research on this tendency, he explained.

Murthy and his team compared a sample of videos that directly recommended official ISIS videos with a random sample of those that did not recommend any radical content and a random sample of YouTube videos. Videos in all three samples were coded for 11 attributes. For example, Murthy explained, all videos were coded as to whether they mentioned social inequalities in the Middle East or whether they were in Arabic. He and his colleagues used an algorithm[10] to identify the relative power of different attributes in identifying the videos that recommended radical content. They found that the attribute that most accurately identified such videos was the use of an explicitly radical keyword (such as ISIS) in the title. This factor, Murthy reported, predicted 35 percent of recommendations. He noted that combinations of attributes offered additional identifications: For example, videos that included content from a newscast, were recent, were in English, and came from an organization rather than an individual were also likely to make radical recommendations. This analysis, he said, showed that YouTube's algorithms for suggesting content to users give high priority to

---

[10] Ragin, C.C., and Davey, S. (2009). *fs/QCA*. Irvine: University of California.

content that is very recent, which may help explain why ISIS bots and individuals continually repost videos. Murthy described his results as somewhat surprising because "it should be really easy for YouTube to figure this out and have filtered this years ago."

DISCUSSION

Following the presentations summarized above, panelists participated in a discussion and responded to audience questions. The discussion revolved around several topics: (1) understanding variability within and across cultures, (2) the impacts of new technology on culture and its role in measurement, and (3) the challenges of measuring cultural phenomena.

Understanding Variability Within and Across Cultures

The importance of investigating culture as a way to understand varying behaviors and actions in context was highlighted in the open discussion. As Dressler pointed out, "the concept of culture has become more important to more people because there is a gap in explanation" for changes in society.

One participant highlighted the need to capture variability within cultures, noting that even individuals can hold conflicting beliefs at the same time. Kahan observed that many people hold simultaneously conflicting beliefs, including scientists whose religious beliefs conflict with their scientific practices. A belief, he explained, is part of a larger cluster of desires, values, and goals that enable people to function in a particular context. In Kahan's view, new research methods are needed to study these conflicts in values.

Murthy explained that he sees culture as socially constructed, created from the collective views that are developed and maintained within a society or social group and from the interaction of different views and ideas within the group. Different social media platforms engender a variety of social media cultures, he asserted, which affect how people behave and express themselves. He gave the example of platforms where people can post anonymously, which often lead to more negative and vitriolic posting. He explained that his work to understand how these online cultures intersect with radicalization focuses on the attributes of anonymous videos that may speak to particular cultural practices. Several cultures interact in these videos, he added, including gaming culture and conservative Islamic culture. He noted further that YouTube cultures are always evolving.

Researchers may have their own views as they seek to interpret the meaning of others' culture, suggested one participant. Dressler said his work focuses intentionally on understanding culture from the perspectives of its members. He explained that even in the face of a high degree of consensus about a domain of culture, his methods enable the identification of contested features and subcultures within a culture. To illustrate this point he cited Brazilian culture, in which working-class families tend to place greater emphasis on the importance of structure, organization, and rules in family life, whereas middle-class families emphasize affective and emotional climate. He added that some of his work on cultural models was conducted and repeated over time, demonstrating the stability of the models. This stability was surprising to him because the transition from a military dictatorship to democracy and the stabilization of the nation's currency occurred within the same 10-year period. However, he noted, his methodology also showed change over time in the lifestyle domain of Brazilian culture; by 2011, information technology (e.g., having a cell phone or Internet access) was emphasized as important for a good life, and traditional face-to-face socializing had decreased in importance.

Kahan argued that while cross-cultural studies are very valuable, researchers need to ensure that the same constructs (e.g., ideas about what is risky) are being measured across the cultures. He explained that he examines the relationships among variables, looking for similarities in patterns across cultures, instead of seeking survey items that might be translated directly from one culture to another. Indicators of a particular attitude vary across cultures, he noted.

Impacts of New Technology

One participant asked the panelists to consider whether technological changes have changed the role of culture. Perhaps the role of culture is shifting from helping people fill gaps in information to helping people filter "noise," he suggested. He speculated that this may be because culture is increasingly self-reinforcing within groups given that so much information is readily available. Kahan explained that in a pluralistic society that is increasingly successful in producing advances in science, a challenging communication environment involving communications among multiple groups who are in conflict with each other becomes more likely. "You add to that the conflict entrepreneur who understands these dynamics too and wants to promote the problem," he said, ". . . therefore, we need even more effective ways of certifying knowledge across these groups." He observed, however, that culture does more than help make people aware of what is known collectively and orient their views around that knowledge; it also fills a basic human need to understand what a good life with others looks like.

Another participant asked the panelists to consider the broader role of the rapidly changing information environment in culture, including whether it is causing an increase in attraction to radical ideologies. Murthy replied that many algorithms operating in online environments, such as those of Amazon and Netflix, are designed to lead to echo chambers—to identify new content that users are likely to be drawn to based on their past choices. In the case of YouTube, he noted, people can begin with innocuous searches and be led to radical content. "Algorithms are value neutral," he said. "If we are making an argument that increasingly our sociocultural dynamics are governed by information communication technologies, which are algorithmically shaped…then we have echo chamber dynamics that we have to largely take into account." He added that these technologies are highly effective from a technical point of view, but they affect polarization and sociocultural dynamics. Weller pointed out that relative to cultural values, attitudes and opinions are more flexible and likely more subject to change and polarization. The information people consume may reinforce attitudes or opinions, she asserted, but not necessarily shift their cultural values.

Murthy also noted that online platforms have some unique features that appear to affect culture. First, he said, the design of the platforms shapes how people engage in the form of likes and comments. He added that these parameters also foster a certain global uniformity: "There is also a certain homogeneity, which I am seeing in my research increasing. That is also partially why ISIS just has to add subtitles on videos. They do not actually have to create new videos for particular cultural contexts, which means that they can be efficacious all around the world." According to Murthy, algorithms in closed platforms are creating some homogeneity in culture, and he added that "from a measurement point of view, it may be a boon because we could then generalize [findings] from a particular cultural context [to other contexts]."

Challenges of Measuring Cultural Phenomena

Dressler observed that the cognitive sciences have made important advances in the ability to conceptualize and measure cultural phenomena by breaking down concepts into manageable components, yet approaches to this research continue to evolve. The amount and types of data sources are changing, noted panel moderator Susan Weller. For example, a participant suggested, changes in the approaches to studying culture may be necessary as people's willingness to participate in survey research declines. Such changes may also necessitate greater reliance on new sources of data, she added. Weller noted further that the availability of large quantities of data enables the use of different approaches, moving away from methods that rely on agreement among individual subjects in their responses to survey questions. Dressler expressed the view that ethnographic approaches that involve working to understand meaning in a culture from the perspective of local individuals will continue to be needed to construct cultural models.

Even with small sample sizes, he asserted, it is possible to identify areas of cultural consensus that are generalizable to the population. He suggested as an interesting area for future research exploring how models uncovered by ethnographic methods could be connected with patterns that can be identified by analyzing large data sources.

Kahan observed that researchers are also seeking the most cost-effective ways to gather data, whether, for example, through such online sources as Mechanical Turk (MTurk),[11] samples recruited through public opinion firms, or random digit dial surveys. However, he emphasized that future research methods should include continually seeking to confirm the validity of different sampling approaches to ensure that studies are accurately reflecting the "real world." He argued that convergent validity based on multiple methods is best, but at the same time, he "would not trust any of our studies if they were not rooted ultimately in the ethnographic methods."

---

[11] See https://www.mturk.com/mturk/welcome [January 2018].

3

Triangulation of Data Sources and Research Methods

Using multiple sources of data and research methods to understand phenomena yields many benefits, explained panel moderator Mark Liberman, University of Pennsylvania. Considering data and findings from multiple sources is valuable, he argued, because doing so serves as a safeguard against being misled by nonrepresentative samples and unreliable research methods. When the goal is to diagnose a problem or predict a future event, he added, using multiple sources of information and multiple methods also leads to more accurate results and conclusions. "As the methods of acquiring data, storing data, and processing data become easier and cheaper," he said, "triangulation becomes a much more efficient thing to do as well as an intellectually better thing to do." Presentations in this panel provided examples of and challenges encountered in triangulating sources and methods in social and behavioral science research.

USING MULTIPLE SOURCES OF DATA TO UNDERSTAND CONFLICT IN ORGANIZATIONS

Giuseppe (Joe) Labianca, University of Kentucky, discussed his research on conflict within organizations, work that entails analyzing networks of people to understand the antecedents and consequences of negative relationships and conflict through the use of survey responses and people's daily communications. He noted that negative relationships in work settings are relatively rare compared with positive and neutral relationships, usually accounting for about 5 percent of the relationships within an organization. However, he added, their rarity can make them very powerful, explaining that people tend to focus on negative relationships and that such relationships have disproportionate effects on performance and other important outcomes in organizations.

In his previous work, Labianca has collected social network data on communication within organizations through surveys after spending time developing trust with an organization's members and meeting with them in small groups. In addition to questions about communication, he explained, these surveys have included questions on how people feel about other members of the organization and the strength of those feelings. He has found, for example, that people may be more willing to answer questions about hearing others' negative gossip than about their own gossiping. Based on the survey responses, Labianca and his team have developed network diagrams and analyses.

Labianca noted that such techniques are useful for organizations of 200 people or fewer, and response rates tend to be very high (85–95%). In large organizations, he said, these same survey methods are not feasible. He went on to describe the methods he employed in studying two large companies that were merging, involving 1,500 corporate professionals. He and his colleagues analyzed many sources of data—e-mails, including both the content of messages and the associated metadata and attachments; survey responses about specific events (e.g., feelings about the recent merger) and about people within the organization and the organization itself; and information from the organization about employee performance, salary, promotions, and turnover.

Labianca reported that to understand conflict resulting from the merger, he and his team worked to develop methods for identifying negative ties from the communication data, rather than through survey responses. From existing qualitative research, the researchers were aware that negative interactions were occurring in the two organizations, including people seeking to undermine others, attempting to get them fired, or spreading disinformation. Prior to the merger, the organizations allowed the research team to talk to one division's new product development group to gather data on members' positive and negative feelings about others in the group.

"Using that set of negative ties that we already [knew] about [from the surveys]," said Labianca, "we [wanted] to use that to try to infer the negative ties in the broader group on top of the four-and-a-half years of qualitative observation and interview data that we already [had]." He added that computational social scientists worked with him to develop ways of using this 150-person dataset as a "training subset" to teach a computer model to infer negative ties in the organizations' larger 1,500-person set. He characterized as a particular challenge that people rarely send negative e-mails directly to individuals with whom they have a conflict, but instead are more likely to send such e-mails to a third person. In addition, he observed, people might not use the name of a person they dislike when complaining about that person to a friend, instead referring to the person obliquely (e.g., "the evil one"). Labianca cited as another challenge the need to identify such conflicts closer to real time. He explained that individuals at the top of an organization usually are not aware of the conflicts at the organization's lower levels, in part because those involved attempt to keep this information from reaching top managers. In the case of the above two merging organizations, he added, individuals involved in leading factional conflicts were ultimately fired, but caused great harm to the organization in the interim.

Ultimately, Labianca and his colleagues would like to be able to use a combination of content, network, attitudinal, and behavioral data to understand negative ties in an organization. These approaches, he explained, can provide important insights into the distribution of power in networks, including who currently has power and who the emerging powerful actors are. Understanding power dependencies is also important, he added, arguing that looking only at alliances within networks often provides an incomplete picture of organizational dynamics.

To illustrate the effects of alliances and adversaries on power dependencies, Labianca described hypothetical power relationships among Egypt, Qatar, Saudi Arabia, and Turkey. When two allies (Egypt and Saudi Arabia) work together against Qatar, he explained, Turkey has more power in the network because Qatar needs its alliance with its sole ally (Turkey) even more given the adversaries it faces. As a result, he continued, Qatar would likely be willing to concede more to Turkey to maintain their alliance. He went on to observe that if Egypt gained another ally, the level of threat to Qatar would increase, further weakening Qatar's power and thereby increasing Turkey's power in the relationship even further. These same dynamics, he added, apply to individuals within organizations, as well as to how countries determine the size of military they need. "As you become more [relationally] powerful as a nation," he elaborated, "you do not need to have as big of a military.[1] That is a simple reaction. Or in the opposite direction, the less powerful you feel [in terms of your network relationship], the more likely you are to grow your military."

Labianca continued by observing that these power dynamics among people in organizations can also yield important information that can explain how individuals with poor performance maintain their positions. He explained that poor-performing individuals can have allies who rely on

---

[1] Smith, J.M., Halgin, D.S., Kidwell-Lopez, V., Labianca, G., Brass, D.J., and Borgatti, S.P. (2014). Power in politically charged networks. *Social Networks*, 36, 162–176. doi:10.1016/j.socnet.2013.04.007.

them more heavily because they have their own adversaries. He and his colleagues have been examining these relationships in varied settings, including among corporate professionals in health care and consulting service organizations. According to Labianca, identifying sources of conflict can help leaders track and mitigate these issues and determine whether their efforts to improve relationships are effective. His research is advancing the development of methods that can be used to understand networks and relationships, going beyond the use of surveys to employ multiple sources of data that can be collected in an unobtrusive manner.

USING DATA FROM SURVEYS, LABORATORY EXPERIMENTS, AND SOCIAL MEDIA TO UNDERSTAND MISINFORMATION

David Broniatowski, The George Washington University, described how using different data sources and research methods can contribute to a better understanding of causality. He explained that methods with high internal validity incorporate designs for identifying causality—Does the proposed treatment cause the proposed effect?—while ruling out other potential explanations for the effect. Alternatively, he continued, external validity is concerned with the extent to which findings are generalizable across settings (e.g., in the laboratory and in the real world). He noted that some methods provide information with high internal validity but low external validity and vice versa, but that triangulation by combining methods is a way to address the shortcomings of any single approach. He asserted that multiple studies using different methods and different data sources can be used to determine whether there are converging lines of evidence to support a theory. He illustrated this multiple-methods approach with his research on the effects of online misinformation on behavior. He emphasized that online misinformation has significant implications for national security because insurgents create different narratives to mobilize certain populations, as documented in military field and counterinsurgency manuals.

According to Broniatowski, online misinformation is also a public health concern, as demonstrated by the role of online narratives in communications about vaccines. Broniatowski and his colleagues examined the effects of narrative framing (the way the choice of words and images of a message affects how it is perceived) on people's decisions. Quoting from a recent article, he said, "Narratives have inherent advantages over other communication formats. . . . They include all of the key elements of memorable messages—they are easy to understand, concrete, credible . . . and highly emotional. These qualities make this type of information compelling

(p. 3730)."[2] Broniatowski used the example of stories conveyed online that describe children getting vaccinated and then developing autism. The gist of these stories, the take-home meaning, he said, is that vaccines cause autism, so that people assume a causal link between the two events when they are merely spuriously correlated.

According to Broniatowski, fuzzy trace theory illuminates how people search for meaning and causal explanations. He explained that this theory posits two types of memory—gist memory for basic meaning and verbatim memory for precise details. It posits further that decisions are based more on gist than on verbatim memory but that the two are encoded in parallel and that both can have an effect on the decisions made. Elaborating on the theory, Broniatowski noted that it also posits that Websites and online content that provide more coherent and meaningful "gists" are more likely to be influential, regardless of whether they are factually accurate, although he added that factual accuracy can have an effect.[3]

The hypotheses of fuzzy trace theory can be tested experimentally, Broniatowski observed. He noted that carefully designed laboratory experiments can have high internal validity because causal relationships between perception and decisions can be identified in controlled conditions. He then described a model for how fuzzy trace theory affects decision making that can be tested in a laboratory setting. First, he said, people are presented with a stimulus (an online narrative), which they then represent in different ways. Specifically, he continued, people encode those messages as precise verbatim facts (e.g., probabilities) and at multiple levels of gist (basic categorical takeaway messages). Each of these representations has a preferred decision outcome determined by a person's values, which are stored in that individual's long-term memory. The various representations are weighted according to that person's personality traits, cognitive needs, competency with numbers, and motivation, among other individual factors. Ultimately, Broniatowski explained, the weightings assigned to the different representations encoded by the individual combine to result in a decision.

According to fuzzy trace theory, Broniatowski explained, the reason people make choices this way is because they interpret numbers in qualitative ways, such as "some" and "none." Most people prefer this type of categorical gist interpretation ("fuzzy processing preference"), he added. He asked the audience to consider the following scenario. An individual must decide which program to adopt. If Program A is adopted, 200 people

---

[2] Betsch, C., Brewer, N.T., Brocard, P., Davies, P., Gaissmaier, W., Haase, N., Leask, J., Renkewitz, F., Renner, B., Reyna, V.F., Rossmann, C., Sachse, K., Schachinger, A., Siegrist, M., and Stryk, M. (2012). Opportunities and challenges of Web 2.0 for vaccination decisions. *Vaccine, 30*(25), 3727–3733.

[3] Reyna, V.F. (2012). Risk perception and communication in vaccination decisions: A fuzzy-trace theory approach. *Vaccine, 30*(25), 3790–3797.

will be saved; if Program B is adopted, there is a one-third probability that 600 people will be saved. In accordance with fuzzy trace theory, the stark categorical contrast between these two options has been eliminated, thereby also eliminating the framing effect. If messages are framed in terms of gain, Broniatowski said, people will choose the possibility of gaining, whereas if messages are framed in terms of loss, people will choose no loss.

Broniatowski and his colleagues tested these predictions using existing data from 30 years' worth of framing and related research and were able to successfully predict choices in 93 percent of studies.[4] In addition, he and his colleagues found other support for their model, providing evidence for the internal validity of their approach for detecting causal effects of framing on decision making.

In parallel, Broniatowski and colleagues tested the extent to which the results of these laboratory experiments were valid under real-world conditions by conducting a survey of patients and health care providers in the Johns Hopkins emergency department about the overuse of antibiotics. The researchers were aware that patients may weigh the choice of whether to take an antibiotic for their illness based on the chance that it might help even if they suspect they have a virus rather than a bacterial infection. "If they do take an antibiotic, given what they know, they may be getting better," Broniatowski added. "They may be staying sick. You can think about this as a categorical framing problem," he explained. His team labeled the gist predicted by fuzzy trace theory "Why not take a risk?"

Broniatowski explained that the survey questions asked respondents to rate the extent to which they agreed with different statements. He and his team then used fuzzy trace theory to test agreement with the "Why not take a risk?" gist and other key messages being tested.[5] Their results supported fuzzy trace theory's predictions, he reported. About three-fourths of patients endorsed the "Why not take a risk?" approach to decision making. Fewer than half of patients endorsed the alternative hypothesis, according to which patients who know the difference between bacteria and viruses will make choices consistent with that knowledge. In fact, Broniatowski observed, most people do not know the difference between the two, and even three-fourths of those that do still endorse the "Why not take a risk?" approach, suggesting that patients still believe it appropriate to take antibiotics even if they probably have symptoms of a virus. Moreover, he added, pilot data suggest that patients who endorse this thinking are also

---

[4] Broniatowski, D.A., and Reyna, V.F. (2017). *A Formal Model of Fuzzy-Trace Theory: Variations on Framing Effects and the Allais Paradox. Decision.* doi:10.1037/dec0000083.

[5] Broniatowski, D.A., Klein, E.Y., and Reyna, V.F. (2015). Germs are germs, and why not take a risk? Patients' expectations for prescribing antibiotics in an inner-city emergency department. *Medical Decision Making, 35*(1), 60–67. doi:10.1177/0272989X14553472.

more likely to expect to receive antibiotics for future illnesses. Finally, he noted, clinicians who endorse "Why not take a risk?" are more likely to prescribe antibiotics.[6]

This study did have some limitations, however, Broniatowski acknowledged. First, he noted, the sample was not nationally representative; it was representative of an urban population of low socioeconomic status and included only a subset of patients who visited the Johns Hopkins emergency department—for example, any patients who were so ill or in pain that they were unable to provide a response were not included. In addition, he observed, those patients surveyed had many different conditions, not just upper respiratory tract infections. Moreover, he emphasized, retrospective observational studies such as this that lack experimental controls for other factors that can affect the behavior(s) of interest (e.g., in this case prescribing behaviors) can have limited validity. Finally, he noted, the study measured beliefs and attitudes, but not behavior.

Another line of Broniatowski's research shows that survey and social media data can be used to cross-validate one another. To understand the spread of misinformation and disinformation online, for example, he and his colleagues examined both news reports and how people shared news about the outbreak of measles at Disneyland in 2014. This outbreak led to 11 cases of measles across several states and Mexico and sparked talk of enacting legislation to toughen vaccination requirements, he reported. He pointed out that individuals involved with public health and health communication would like to better understand whether providing facts or using narrative storytelling, or some combination of the two, is the most effective and ethical way to communicate messages designed to increase vaccination rates.

According to Broniatowski, fuzzy trace theory suggests that people encode both facts and gist in parallel. In the case of vaccination, he continued, the facts are the statistics about vaccination and the gist is the basic meaning—vaccination is the best way to protect your child. As he explained, "Stories are effective to the extent that they communicate a gist that cues motivationally relevant, moral, and social principles." He and his colleagues coded about 4,500 articles to examine measles coverage on social media. Using the Facebook application programming interface (API), they measured how frequently those articles were shared, and using MTurk, they examined whether the articles included statistics about viruses or vaccines. In addition, they coded for whether the article had a gist or "bottom-line

---

[6]Klein, E.Y., Martinez, E.M., May, L., Saheed, M., Reyna, V., and Broniatowski, D.A. (2017). Categorical risk perception drives variability in antibiotic prescribing in the emergency department: A mixed methods observational study. *Journal of General Internal Medicine*, 32(10), 1083–1089. doi:10.1007/s11606-017-4099-6.

meaning," and controlled for other covariates based on prior literature. To ensure reliable coding, they used multiple coders and measured interrater reliability. Broniatowski observed that one advantage of using social media data is the lack of response bias that can occur when people know they are participating in a survey. In the case of this research, he asserted, the data represent people's actual behaviors without any researcher intervention.

Broniatowski explained that the results of this research were consistent with the predictions of fuzzy trace theory. When an article conveyed a gist, he reported, it was 2.3 times more likely to be shared at least once relative to articles not containing a gist. Articles with statistics were also 1.3 times more likely to be shared than articles without statistics, but less so than those with a gist. No significant effects were observed for articles that conveyed a story but had no effective gist. Broniatowski added that among articles shared more than once, those that communicated positive opinions about both sides of the vaccination debate but then concluded with a recommended course of action and communicated a gist were shared, on average, 58 times more often than other articles.

Broniatowski emphasized that converging lines of evidence increase confidence in the conclusions of research, as one research approach can address the limitations of another. In the case of the research he described, he said, results across multiple settings, populations, and research methods support fuzzy trace theory's predictions. He plans future work to examine the mechanisms that influence the decision to share an article and how this process influences an information cascade, in which people's decisions are influenced by observing the behavior of others in combination with their own personal information.

CHALLENGES IN TRIANGULATING HEALTH CARE DATA

According to Philip Resnik, University of Maryland, natural language processing (NLP) combined with methodology from computational social science and triangulated with other sources of data can be applied to better understand the types of health issues that can affect national security. National security can be compromised if there are too few healthy young people to recruit, he noted, or if potential recruits see that veterans receive inadequate care for the aftereffects of war.[7] Outside of the military, he continued, increased rates of suicide and opioid addiction force the nation to focus on these internal issues more than on foreign affairs and external threats.

---

[7] Brooks, M. (2016). Want new recruits? Take care of the old ones. *Modern War Institute at West Point*, November 11. Available: https://mwi.usma.edu/want-new-recruits-take-care-old-ones [February 2018].

Using behavior to draw inferences about a population or individuals is a method with potentially broad application, Resnik observed. For example, he explained, many kinds of behavior can be thought of as a vote—a binary choice between options. Examples of ways in which people cast votes, he said, are "if you have a mechanism for real-time responses where people can say I agree or disagree with what I am hearing during a debate, or if you are looking at the Twitter stream where people are expressing positive or negative sentiment about something."[8] He noted that models of the voting behavior of legislators reflect this by taking into account drivers of their behavior, such as the popularity of a policy choice. He argued that although some models can show how behaviors map to liberal and conservative ideology, identifying themes associated with closely related terms from the language used in bills and speeches on the floor of Congress provides a richer source of data for explaining the influences of language on voting behavior. He and his colleagues showed that the words used to discuss topics frame issues in ways that help better predict how legislators will vote.[9]

Resnik presented a model of how different linguistic terms used during the discussion of the debt ceiling differentiated Tea Party Republicans from those who more represented the "establishment" wing of the Republican party (see Figure 3-1). This model includes two levels: agenda issues and framing of those issues. At one level (the top portion of the figure), the words cluster around macroeconomic issues, such as "balanced budget," "national debt," and "grandchildren." However, Resnik noted, the framing of the Republican "establishment" (M1) tends to include terms that represent more practical considerations in that debate, such as "government shutdown" and "blame," whereas the Tea Party framing (M3) emphasizes terms associated with party principles, such as "entitlements," "debt," and "taxes."

The second level of framing in Figure 3-1 illustrates how similar analyses using NLP can be applied to understanding issues in health care and mental health, including depression and suicidality, by examining how people frame issues in their conversations. "For example," Resnik said, "two people can be talking about [their] schedules. But [one] might be

---

[8] Argyle, D., Resnik, P., and Eidelman, V. (2016). *Using Ideal Point Models to Characterize Political Reactions in Non-Political Actors*. Presented at Seventh Annual Conference on New Directions in Analyzing Text as Data, Northeastern University, October 14.

[9] Nguyen, V.-A., Boyd-Graber, J., Resnik, P., and Miler, K. (2015). Tea Party in the house: A hierarchical ideal point topic model and its application to Republican legislators in the 112th Congress. In *Proceedings of the 53rd Annual Meeting of the Association for Computational Linguistics and the 7th International Joint Conference on Natural Language Processing* (pp. 1438–1448). Beijing, China: Association for Computational Linguistics. Available: https://aclanthology.info/pdf/P/P15/P15-1139.pdf [February 2018].

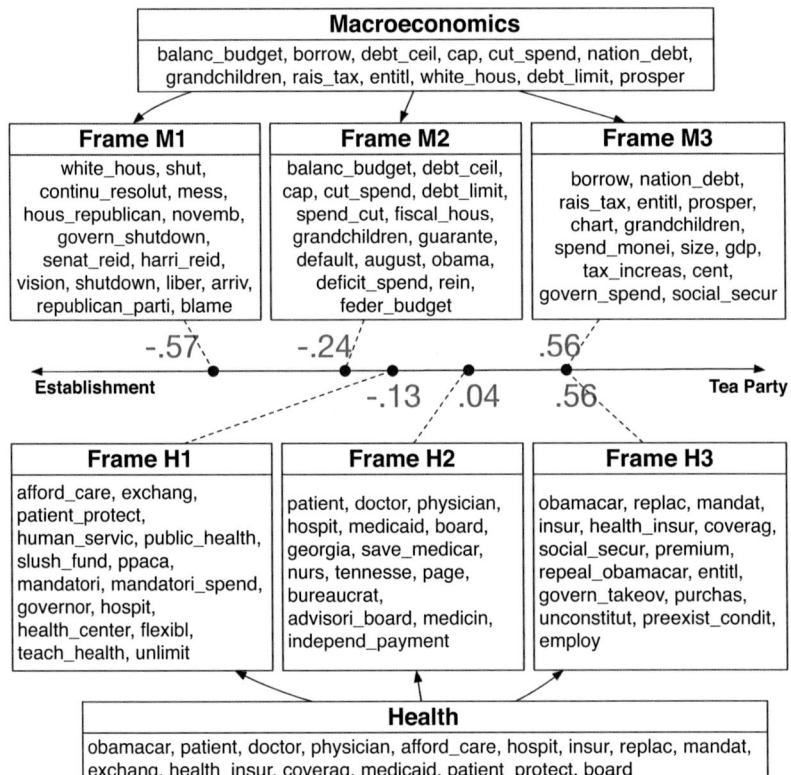

FIGURE 3-1 Republican framing of macroeconomics and health care in the 112th Congress.
NOTE: The material above the line models the connection between ideological position and linguistic framing in floor debate on macroeconomics; the parallel information below the line models that connection in the context of health care. The horizontal line represents a spectrum of Republican ideology from more "establishment" oriented (left) to more "Tea Party" oriented (right).
SOURCE: Nguyen, V.-A., Boyd-Graber, J., Resnik, P., and Miler, K. (2015). Tea Party in the house: A hierarchical ideal point topic model and its application to Republican legislators in the 112th Congress. In *Proceedings of the 53rd Annual Meeting of the Association for Computational Linguistics and the 7th International Joint Conference on Natural Language Processing* (pp. 1438–1448, fig. 6). Beijing, China: Association for Computational Linguistics. Available: https://aclanthology.info/pdf/P/P15/P15-1139.pdf [February 2018]. Reprinted with permission from the Association for Computational Linguistics.

expressing it in terms of looking forward to the weekend, and [the other] might be expressing it in terms of how exhausted [he or she] is when getting up in the morning." He added that studies testing this idea have found that such differences in the way people talk can predict mental health concerns.[10]

NLP has been growing as a discipline for roughly 40 years, Resnik observed, and since the early 1990s, it has been on the leading edge of machine learning and applied to understanding a variety of phenomena. Currently, he noted, NLP research can make use of a variety of large datasets. He illustrated this point with examples of publicly available datasets including 1.6 million tweets, 681,288 social media posts, more than 140 million words from online bloggers, and one terabyte-sized dataset containing every publicly available Reddit comment as of 2015.[11] However, he argued, the state of the art for NLP in medical or clinical settings is about 10 years behind that for NLP in other application areas because available datasets in the health care domain are far fewer and much smaller. He gave examples of orders-of-magnitude differences in data availability, including one dataset from the Mayo Clinic containing 400 manually deidentified clinical notes and pathology reports from cancer patients and another dataset containing 65,000 posts from a mental health peer support forum. The limited number of records available, he asserted, fails to provide the "ground truth" sought by researchers of large datasets. He called attention to one recent improvement, the MIMIC (Multiparameter Intelligent Monitoring in Intensive Care) dataset with data from about 40,000 intensive care unit patients (albeit from just one medical center), which includes 2 million free-text clinical notes.[12]

According to Resnik, several problems contribute to the limitations of NLP in health research. First, he asserted, privacy laws with respect to health information discourage sharing of this information, which results in balkanizing research. Second, he said, linguistic data, compared with other health data, are difficult to fully deidentify. Even if as much as 99 percent of the data can be deidentified, he observed, the remaining 1 percent that

---

[10] Resnik, P., Armstrong, W., Claudino, L., Nguyen, T., Nguyen, V.-A., and Boyd-Graber, J. (2015). Beyond LDA: Exploring supervised topic modeling for depression-related language in Twitter. In *Proceedings of the 2nd Workshop on Computational Linguistics and Clinical Psychology: From Linguistic Signal to Clinical Reality* (pp. 99–107). Denver, CO: Association for Computational Linguistics. Available: http://www.aclweb.org/anthology/W/W15/W15-1212.pdf [February 2018].

[11] See https://www.reddit.com/r/datasets/comments/3bxlg7/i_have_every_publicly_available_reddit_comment [February 2018].

[12] Johnson, A.E.W., Pollard, T.J., Shen, L., Lehman, L.H., Feng, M., Ghassemi, M., Moody, B., Szolovits, P., Celi, L.A., and Mark, R.G. (2016). MIMIC-III, a freely accessible critical care database. *Scientific Data, 3*, 160035. doi:10.1038/sdata.2016.35.

cannot be is problematic given the millions of records involved. Finally, he said, electronic health records create pressure to avoid language because the new systems encourage the use of pull-down menus and checkboxes instead of recording of narrative clinical data. All of these barriers, he argued, discourage NLP researchers, who simply choose other topics to research. He asserted that addressing these barriers will require policy, not technical, solutions.

Resnik identified data donation as one approach to increasing the amount of health data available to researchers. He reported that one company, Qntfy, maintains a Website, OurDataHelps.org, that enables people to donate private social media data for mental health research (Qntfy anonymizes the data for research use and provides a consent structure). Taking approaches of this kind, he explained, would address the constraints imposed by the Health Insurance Portability and Accountability Act of 1996 (HIPAA) because it allows individuals to control their own health information. The founder of Qntfy, Glen Coppersmith, has used such data to study suicidality and other conditions, and Resnik is collaborating with Coppersmith (and Deanna Kelly at the University of Maryland School of Medicine) to take the same data donation approach in studying schizophrenia and depression.

Resnik concluded by suggesting that such repositories for data could be scaled up. He cited the University of Pennsylvania Linguistic Data Consortium, the National Institutes of Health's (NIH's) Precision Medicine Initiative,[13] and other collaborations as examples of efforts to compile donated data for research, including NLP research. Although the NIH initiative is a very large project aimed at collecting donated data from 1 million people, he added, the early focus is not on collecting language data, because it is challenging to collect and deidentify such data. He ended by saying, "Language data as part of what you triangulate along with behavioral data and structure data, metadata, and so forth, is an enormously important resource, but we have a lot of catching up to do, and more needs to be done faster."

DISCUSSION

Following the panel presentations, workshop participants discussed some of the ideas raised. The discussion, moderated by Mark Liberman, focused on several themes: (1) the need for methods that are adaptable, timely, and rigorous; (2) communicating with decision makers and building trust; (3) roles and limitations of automated and human data analysis; and (4) investments in data sources and data sharing.

---

[13] See http://www.allofus.nih.gov [February 2018].

Need for Adaptability, Speed, and Rigor

One participant from the Intelligence Community (IC) noted that in that community, methods need to be adaptable to new situations and data sources, produce timely results, and be rigorous enough to provide confidence in the findings. Two panelists discussed the trade-offs of speed and rigor and ways to address them. Resnik said, "So much of what we do as data-driven scientists involves developing automatic methods, but I am firmly convinced that when you want to do things in the real world, you need to spend more time focusing on the human in the loop." He added that the combination of automation and human analysis balances bottom-up approaches, in which conclusions are reached based on patterns that emerge from the data collected, and top-down approaches, in which humans help define categories used to interpret these patterns. When the two approaches are used together, he asserted, the limitations of either alone are balanced, lending confidence to the results.

Broniatowski noted that each method comes with pros and cons that must be weighed against the primary considerations of the researchers. For example, he observed, social media data can be collected very quickly, but rigorous methods for their analysis comparable to survey research methods have not yet been established. Alternatively, he suggested, when rapid results are required, such as during an outbreak of infectious disease, using a rigorously designed survey of people's understanding and actions might not produce results in time, even if it yields robust findings. For these reasons, he argued, both researchers and consumers of research should be aware of the trade-offs entailed in selecting one approach over another. He added that being able to communicate these trade-offs and the nature of uncertainty to decision makers is of critical importance. This means, he elaborated, that analysts need to be clear on the central message, the gist, that they want to convey about the data while accurately portraying the degree of confidence in that message in an understandable way.

Broniatowski and Liberman also addressed the need for methods adaptable to new questions and contexts. Broniatowski explained that flexibility can be built into the structures that govern the flow of information in organizations, suggesting that resources and research are available to guide the examination and design of such structures. Liberman stated that the issue of generalizability—whether findings from one context hold true in another—is linked to the issue of communicating clearly to instill confidence in decision makers.

Communicating with Decision Makers and Building Trust

Several panelists and participants discussed how to communicate research findings to decision makers and the importance of trust in data sources, methods, findings, and communicators. A participant from the IC suggested that reducing barriers between academic work and decision makers through effective communication is one means of building trust, especially under conditions of uncertainty. He added that conveying the gist of the research, transparently and honestly, includes stating the limits of current knowledge and understanding and conveying uncertainty in ways people understand. Uncertainty and risk make people uncomfortable, he asserted, and being able to "tell a story with those concepts that imbues trust, I think that is the mechanism for going from the theoretical world to the applied world."

Broniatowski explained that determining the gist to be conveyed sometimes requires particular expertise. A person who understands the methodology of researchers as well as the concerns of decision makers is the ideal expert for translating research, he argued. Often, he added, those skilled at data analysis are not skilled at communicating and vice versa, so he suggested considering utilizing people who can serve in translational roles.

Resnik agreed that having individuals serve in translational roles could help address the significant gap that often exists between analysts and the people their research is intended to serve in the national security contexts in which he works. In his view, more attention should be paid to developing better connections between technology or analytic models and the problems they are intended to help solve. He added that some mistakes erode trust in the system even if the system is accurate 99 percent of the time. He argued that avoiding those types of errors is essential for maintaining trust.

One participant noted that the source of data or of funding for research can contribute to a lack of trust in the conclusions of the research. For example, she has encountered situations in which research conducted or published outside the United States was considered potentially biased or suspect. In her experience, there has also been a tendency not to trust research unless it was funded by the Defense Advanced Research Projects Agency (DARPA), the Intelligence Advanced Research Projects Activity (IARPA), or other similar sources. She noted that this has had the effect of limiting the research considered potentially useful and suggested that triangulation could be one strategy for increasing confidence in the findings from these underutilized sources. Liberman noted that in his experience, DARPA- and IARPA-funded research has long been international, and researchers have utilized promising results from other countries.

Resnik suggested that authority based on a certain funding source no longer need be a basis for trust, particularly when datasets and codes for analyzing them are increasingly available so that results can be verified and replicated. More peer review processes and conferences are valuing this type of transparency, he explained. He added that adhering to rigorous scientific methods and replicating results in multiple settings, including within and outside of the United States, can increase trust in the results.

The Roles and Limitations of Automated and Human Data Analysis

Participants also discussed the importance of both automated and human data analysis in social and behavioral science research. Labianca explained that although he is able to employ computers to examine e-mail content and survey data and to develop models for predicting behavior, these automated methods cannot produce an answer for why the models work. Liberman added that "the trend in our field broadly construed over the last few years is toward theories that work better and better and are explainable less and less. I think that is a challenge for the next decade." Resnik noted that this trend is spawning an industry aimed at explaining these models and important aspects of data.

Other participants agreed that the human role in making meaning out of data is vital. For example, one participant suggested, an algorithm may assign a particular meaning to a pattern of data, but a person is still important for determining whether the algorithm assigned the correct meaning. Labianca explained that in NLP, punctuation and emojis can be important indicators of meaning, but that meanings associated with these symbols can differ in complex ways (e.g., an exclamation point can indicate that someone is yelling or that someone is pleased). He emphasized that understanding the true nature of interactions is essential for developing a theoretical explanation for phenomena. Resnik continued the discussion by identifying two components of meaning: the first is a representation that can be manipulated to accomplish the second—reasoning about the meaning, drawing inferences and conclusions, and making decisions.

Broniatowski explained that understanding the gist of a message necessarily means understanding the contextualized meaning. In his view, there is increasing recognition that to make sense of the data, the analyst must also understand the algorithms used to gather the data. He argued that analysts who understand both the algorithms and national security needs can better discern important meaning in the context of particular problems. "I think the royal road to doing that in a sense is to make sure that in addition to improving our analysis techniques, we are also making sure that we are improving our expertise in the interpretation of those techniques," he said. Resnik agreed, emphasizing that in his view, humans will continue to fill these gaps in interpretation for "quite some time." At the same time, he asserted, the data analysis field needs to advance toward systems that create more meaningful representations useful for drawing inferences and answering fundamental research questions.

Investments in Data Sources and Data Sharing

Several participants emphasized the need for investments in data over the next decade. Labianca argued that mechanisms are needed to facilitate the secure sharing of deidentified data among universities or other research institutions. Liberman agreed, noting that these issues are especially sensitive and challenging when it comes to health data, and asserting that solutions will require both legal and procedural attention. He added that determining the most appropriate ways to share medical, organizational, and social media data for legitimate research purposes will require a great deal more discussion.

Broniatowski expanded on this idea, noting that data sharing can be considered one layer of a hierarchy. This layer is important, he said, because different people can examine the data and reach different conclusions. However, he also suggested that sharing interpretations of data and their relationship to decisions is another layer of the hierarchy that should be considered. He cited as an important investment establishing infrastructure across intelligence agencies to enable communication and lateral connections allowable by law at multiple levels—the data level, the level of interpretation of the data, and the decision-making level based on the interpretation.

Labianca suggested that incentives for sharing data should also be considered because some organizations, such as health insurance and social media companies, possess important data. He also emphasized the importance of bridging the gap between data and knowledge. With the current advances and interest in machine- and data-driven learning, he argued, more attention should be paid to using knowledge, such as meaningful categories and the relationships among them, to improve models and the understanding of phenomena.

4

The Challenge of Multiple Levels of Analysis

Panel moderator David Matsumoto, San Francisco State University, opened this session by observing that various social and behavioral science disciplines often focus on different units of analysis, ranging from individuals and small groups to societies or cultures. These differences, he asserted, pose challenges to researchers because concepts or findings at one level of analysis may not translate to other levels. "When we are [looking] at the broad spectrum of social science research related to the question of changing social cultural dynamics and its implications for people's behaviors," he said, "one question then becomes, What is the relationship between what you find at a macro-social level [and] predicting people's behaviors and vice versa? We can understand people's behaviors, and we may or may not understand what the macro-social dynamics are like." Following Matsumoto's introductory remarks, the session included presentations on levels of influence, patterns of cultural variation, and levels of analysis and linguistics. These presentations were followed by discussion and concluding remarks for the workshop.

LEVELS OF INFLUENCE

Gwyneth Sutherlin, Geographic Services, Inc., suggested that methods ranging from ethnographic fieldwork to the use of artificial intelligence could allow social science research to provide significant advances in understanding patterns of human behavior and culture. In her view, however, social science methods can be improved to increase the richness of data and possibilities for collaboration with other disciplines and also to better address national security questions.

Although trained as a mechanical engineer, Sutherlin noted, she now researches how discrete technological advances can allow forward progression in political science and conflict analysis. Thus, her work has focused on issues of conflict among communities around the world. She has sought to understand the difficult-to-define characteristics of the cultures of communities based on how their members understand themselves, as well as the characteristics that define these communities in relation to others with which they are in conflict. Among the many characteristics of a culture, she focuses only on those that are the source of conflict, then operationalizes them so that they are observable and discrete and can inform decision making with respect to conflict and peace.

Increasingly, Sutherlin noted, new technologies are being applied to collect these cultural data. However, she has observed a disconnect between the data she collects on the ground and the analytic output to inform decision making. She highlighted the need to enrich understanding of places outside the United States "linguistically in terms of how other cultures think and understand their environment, problem solve, strategize, [and] have different time event horizons" based on what is encountered in the field and in the data collected.

In her role at Geographic Services, Inc., Sutherlin directs the development of technology that enables examination of large datasets following the same rigorous processes she applies in her fieldwork. The technology uses interactive graph databases with multiple variables, she explained, enabling her and other researchers to scale rich, robustly validated data from the neighborhood level to the country and regional levels. According to Sutherlin, this capability can provide a diverse picture of a particular scenario, and, she added, these rich sociocultural data can also provide a training set for machine learning.

Sutherlin then described ways in which these data could be further enriched. For example, she pointed out, languages spoken in a particular area can be depicted graphically on a map. She argued that maps illustrating the many other primary languages around the world underscore the need to better understand these cultures on their own terms, especially given the dominant focus on English and closely related European languages in academic research. This focus, she asserted, has the limited understanding of linguistics and how other cultures function and also limited the usefulness of software and analytic systems that rely on English-language data sources for training.

Sutherlin continued by observing that applying principles and theories from one culture to similar phenomena in another can be problematic. She cited the example of the application of lessons learned about how people joined gangs in Chicago during the 1930s to understanding ISIS recruitment. "I think it is reasonable to question if that should be applied outside the U.S. in the 21st century to non-Americans," she cautioned. "There are many theories like this that people do not [examine] critically. . . ." In other words, she asserted, theories applied to solving problems need to be culturally adapted.

According to Sutherlin, knowledge of how language works around the world is quite limited, and language universals have yet to be discovered. In addition, she observed, researchers know little about language on online platforms, which presents both a problem and an opportunity. She explained that cultures can differ greatly in how they think, including their concepts of time; concepts of location, number, and counting; and whether and how they use categorization. In addition, she said, they may differ in how they conceptualize events in ways that are important to understanding their narratives. She gave the example of the way in which members of a culture explain who was part of an event and the causes and effects of the event, all of which can be highly culturally specific. "That construction of how people perceive, remember, and recall an event is completely different," she argued. "Not language by language, but culture by culture. We are not able to contend with that with our current [data] collection and analysis. That is a huge area for development," she asserted.

Whether intentionally programmed or unintentionally encoded, Sutherlin continued, algorithms and analytic software encode social theories and assumptions. Often, she explained, these systems separate information based only on language, and that process is frequently imperfect. At other times, she noted, proxy variables for culture are used, but these variables are difficult for software developers to identify. She argued that concepts derived from the way cultures understand themselves should drive software models so that analytics are specific to each area researchers and others want to understand.

According to Sutherlin, promising directions for addressing the limitations of how cultures around the world are understood include starting small with well-researched and field-based cultural concepts before pairing these approaches with other methodologies. She emphasized the need for more research on the particular languages and dialects used in various places. She cited the example of Iraq, where three separate Kurdish dialects are used, yet many groups working to understand Iraq remain unaware of such differences. She believes that ultimately, interactive, culturally based models aided by technology can help address such gaps in understanding of different cultures around the world. One promising approach, she suggested, is "putting a lot of these social and culture factors in a graph database, which allows you to take very small data and scale them out in a large network."

PATTERNS OF CULTURAL VARIATION

Michele J. Gelfand, University of Maryland, College Park, discussed her approaches to integrating multiple levels of analysis across different disciplines in her work as a cross-cultural psychologist studying the tightness and looseness of controls and norms of behavior. She looks for patterns across these levels while recognizing the distinct causes and consequences of phenomena within each level.

Gelfand has observed differences across cultures in how tightly behavior is constricted by the rules and norms of the society. For example, she pointed out, Singapore has a culture with many rules, and its citizens can be fined for flying a kite or spitting in a public place; in New Zealand, by contrast, people walk into public buildings barefoot, and rules are more relaxed and more eccentric behavior tolerated. She added that similar contrasts can be observed among cities around the world in, for example, observance of traffic laws, control and acceptance of marijuana use, and even patterns of how parents choose to name their children. "What ties these together, in my view, are that they are all related to social norms, these standards of behavior that we share in certain human groups," she said.

Gelfand explained that these norms are the "glue" that keeps cultures together and that having such norms is universal. Humans are expert at developing, following, and enforcing social norms, she observed, especially across generations. However, she added, cultures differ greatly in the strength of that social "glue"—how tight or loose the social norms are in any particular group across different levels of analysis. Tight groups have strong norms and strong punishments for deviance, she explained, while loose groups have weaker norms and a higher degree of permissiveness. She noted that such differences have been observed worldwide even since ancient times.

Gelfand has studied this phenomenon of tightness and looseness at the level of the individual, within social classes, in organizations, and across modern nations and states. Ecological factors and historical events influence the social organization of a country, she observed, which in turn affects the characteristics of social situations and associated psychological processes.[1] She suggested that this is one way of modeling culture across different levels of analysis. Her research has focused on how the broad historical, ecological, social, and political institutions of a society affect cultural concerns about norms and how these norms then influence everyday behavior (see Figure 4-1). For this research, she has identified 33 countries across six continents based on her theoretical predictions and recruited a sample of nearly 7,000 participants, who spoke 22 different languages. She gathered

---

[1] Triandis, H.C. (1972). *The Analysis of Subjective Culture*. New York: Wiley.

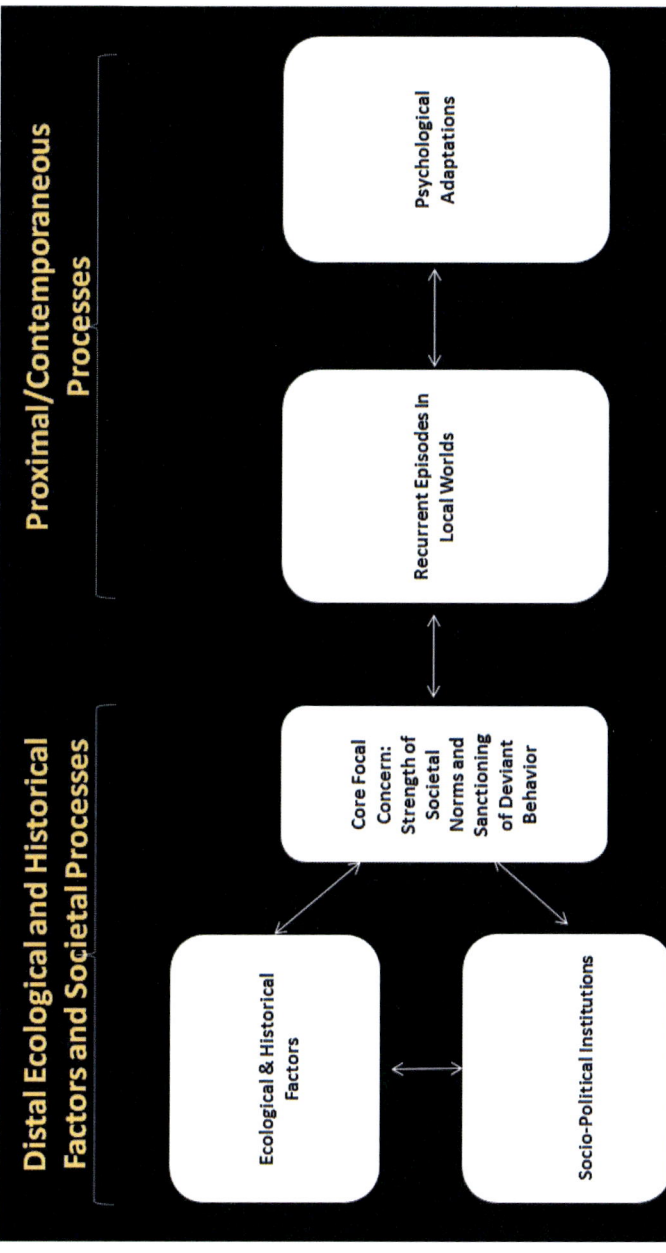

FIGURE 4-1 Model of a tightness–looseness system.
SOURCE: Gelfand, M.J., Raver, J.L., Nishii, L., Leslie, L.M., Lun, J., Lim, B.C., Duan, L., Almaliach, A., Ang, S., Arnadottir, J., Aycan, Z., et al. (2011). Differences between tight and loose cultures: A 33-nation study. *Science, 332*(6033), 1100–1104, fig. 1. doi:10.1126/science.1197754. Reprinted with permission from *Science*, American Association for the Advancement of Science (Copyright Clearance Center).

survey data from these participants and collected ecological and historical data. In addition, her research team conducted unobtrusive observations of behavior in public settings.

As Figure 4-1 illustrates, Gelfand's tightness–looseness system can be understood as part of a larger complex, loosely integrated system involving processes across multiple levels of analysis. Her research indicated that people can agree on the degree of tightness or looseness of the norms in their society when asked. Further, she observed, the tightness–looseness construct was distinct from participants' ideas about collectivism and other factors related to the economic state of their society. She added that both tight and loose societies enable multiple levels of analysis that convey the trade-offs people perceive within each type.

According to Gelfand, tight cultures have greater order and predictability. They have more security and cleaning personnel and have less crime, generally speaking. Tighter cultures display greater uniformity in cars and clothing, and have more synchronous clocks and even more synchronous stock markets,[2] she noted. By contrast, loose cultures are more disorganized, have more crime, and have less synchrony. However, loose cultures are characterized by more openness, less cultural superiority, less ethnocentrism, and more acceptance of immigrants and people who tend to be stigmatized (e.g., immigrants, homosexuals, people with tattoos).

Gelfand explained that her research is aimed at identifying factors that predict this tightness or looseness. Gross domestic product, common religion, language, and geographic location do not serve this purpose, she stated. One the other hand, common threats experienced by countries and groups—such as territorial invasions, natural disasters, food scarcity, dense population, and prevalent pathogens—can serve as a strong impetus for coordination and organization that help societies survive. Accordingly, her data show a strong connection between these threats and tightness or looseness, controlling for gross national product per capita. Gelfand cited the example of Singapore, a very densely populated country with three dominant groups, noting that the tightness of its culture helps prevent conflict among these groups living so closely together. She explained that people in Singapore agree to tighter controls because they feel secure in return. "In the context of high threat," she said, "you can sacrifice liberty for some security. In a context where you have very little threat or less threat, then you prioritize freedom over security."

At another level of analysis, Gelfand examines the strength or weakness of the controls on behavior in certain social situations. Situations with strong controls on behavior, such as being in a library or attending

---

[2] Eun, C.S., Wang, L., and Xiao, S.C. (2015). Culture and R^2. *Journal of Financial Economics, 115*(2), 283–303.

a funeral, allow for little variation in behavior, and behavior that violates norms is likely to be censured. On the other hand, Gelfand explained, situations with weak controls on behavior, such as being in a public park or in one's home, allow for a wider range of behavior. She noted that people negotiate both types of situations throughout daily life, but that people in tight cultures experience a greater preponderance of situations with strong controls. These cultural effects can be observed at the individual level, she added. People who live in tight cultures focus more on prevention, regulate their own behavior, and desire structure to a greater extent relative to people in loose cultures, she elaborated. By contrast, people in loose cultures focus more on promotion and have a higher tolerance for ambiguity compared with people in tight cultures. Gelfand added that, as opposed to thinking of individuals as tight or loose, she sees people as adapting individually to situations with strong or weak controls on behavior.

Gelfand has also explored variability within countries, within organizations, and within social classes with respect to tightness and looseness by examining survey and archival data. She reported that findings from this research in the United States indicate that southern states are tightest, coastal states are loosest, and the remaining states vary in this regard.[3] Tightness, she noted, is predicted by amount of food insecurity, proneness to natural disaster, disease stress, and how rural the state is. The consequences of this tightness, she said, include more organization, more law enforcement, less homelessness, and less divorce, as well as more self-control, less drug abuse, and less debt. Looser states are on the other end of the spectrum on those same factors, she added, and their openness is also associated with greater creativity. Thus these states are characterized by more patents and fine artists per capita, more equality and fewer equal employment opportunity claims, and more minority businesses.

Gelfand and her collaborator, Jesse Harrington, have also examined differences in tightness and looseness among people from different social classes. In this research, they were seeking to determine whether members of a lower social class perceived themselves to be under threat in a pattern similar to that of people in countries threatened by conflict or natural disasters. According to Gelfand, working-class families worry about falling into poverty or being the victim of crime. They also, she noted, typically work in more dangerous professions that require following rules to a greater extent relative to people in middle-class environments, which display more emphasis on creativity. She added that families often raise their children to fit into their environments.

Gelfand described results she and Harrington derived from a survey

---

[3] Harrington, J.R., and Gelfand, M.J. (2014). Tightness–looseness across the 50 united states. *Proceedings of the National Academy of Sciences, 111*(22), 7990–7995.

of 300 working- and middle-class adults, on which working-class adults reported greater tightness and more positive attitudes toward rules compared with middle-class adults. She and Harrington also measured threat by linking zip codes to indexes of poverty and unemployment. Patterns of psychological characteristics of working-class families (e.g., need for structure, conscientiousness) were consistent with national-level data. Additional studies with larger, representative samples have replicated these findings, Gelfand noted. She added that differences in reactions to norm violations enacted by puppets in a laboratory setting could be observed in children as young as 3 years old. Middle-class children tended to find the puppets' rule breaking funny, whereas working-class children asked the puppets to stop and more often saw the behavior as wrong.

Gelfand and her colleagues also examined neural data to determine whether cultural differences and norm violations produce any visible changes in the brain. They explored whether any such changes were related to outcomes they had observed at other levels of analysis, such as self-control, ethnocentrism, or creativity. In this research, they examined the brain responses of individuals in the United States and China 400 milliseconds after being presented with a stimulus (referred to in neuroscience as the N400 response). Some of these stimuli were strong norm violations (e.g., a person dancing in an art museum), but others violated norms weakly or not at all (e.g., a person dancing in the park or during a tango lesson). As expected, Gelfand reported, the brain activity of people from both cultures showed stronger reactions to strong norm violations than to other stimuli. However, she added, the two groups showed differing responses in the frontal area of the brain when asked such questions as "Why did someone do this?" or "What should we do about this behavior?" She suggested that these differences, in turn, were related to self-control, creativity, and feelings of cultural superiority.

Another line of Gelfand's research is beginning to examine linkages between perceived societal threat and the speed of brain synchrony between people. Theory predicts, she explained, that people who perceive a threat develop strong norms needed to coordinate social action. In this research, she and her team measured the coordination of brain waves of pairs of subjects under three different conditions representing ingroup threat, outgroup threat, and no threat. They then measured pairs' coordination on a counting task while in separate rooms. Gelfand reported that under high ingroup threat, the pairs showed more behavioral coordination, related in part to the synchrony of their brain wave activity.

Gelfand explained further that the threat people perceive can also be manipulated and activated subjectively. Before the November 2016 election, she and her colleagues measured the perceived threat from such groups as ISIS, North Korea, and immigrants; belief about whether the country was too loose; the desire for greater tightness; and whether these perceptions and feelings predicted voting for Donald Trump among a representative sample of 500 Americans. According to Gelfand, the results of these measurements were in line with predictions: perceived threat was positively related to desire for greater tightness, which in turn was positively related to voting for Trump. She and her team replicated this study in France to predict voting for Le Pen, a far-right presidential candidate. This dynamic is not a modern phenomenon, she added.

Gelfand concluded by reporting research findings indicating that neither extreme looseness nor extreme tightness is healthy,[4] noting that both of these extremes are related to higher depression and suicidality, higher blood pressure, and lower happiness. "I think what this suggests to us," she said, "is that we need to be thinking about this dimension in terms of what is happening around the world, when groups [have] these pendulum shifts from very tight to very loose and back to tight again. This happened in Egypt in the Arab Spring," she added, "where you went from very tight culture where you got rid of this top-down control. Without any ability to self-organize and synchronize, we could see that people desire the same kind of autocracy that they had in the first place, what we call autocratic recidivism. We can show that with data." She noted that her team's research in Egypt after Mubarak was overthrown confirmed this pattern.

LEVELS OF ANALYSIS AND LINGUISTICS

Computer algorithms provide an important way to learn about language, explained Jesse Egbert, Northern Arizona University, but they must remain interpretable. At times, he observed, maintaining interpretability means omitting variables he cannot explain, which reduces to some extent the ability to predict outcomes of interest. However, he said, any predictive accuracy that is lost is more than made up for by an increase in the ability to explain the patterns identified by computers. Without this interpretability, he added, computational linguistic research often raises more questions than it answers, especially with large datasets. Referencing Nate Silver's book *The Signal and the Noise*,[5] Egbert stated that the ability to distinguish "signal," or meaningful patterns, from "noise" may be declining, despite the fact that people have access to more data than ever before via the Internet. He proposed that preserving linguistic interpretability in computational linguistics is one way researchers can counter this trend.

---

[4]Harrington, J.R., Boski, P., and Gelfand, M.J. (2015). Culture and national well-being: Should societies emphasize freedom or constraint? *PLOS ONE*, *10*(6), e0127173.

[5]Silver, N. (2012). *The Signal and the Noise: Why So Many Predictions Fail—But Some Don't*. New York: Penguin.

Egbert suggested that a corpus, or large sample of texts, is like a forest. This forest, he said, can be thought of as a single unit, but it also comprises individual "trees" or texts, independent units of naturally occurring language (e.g., a conversation or a workshop presentation) that have a beginning and an end and serve a function. Like individual trees in a forest, he continued, these texts are made up of smaller parts—linguistic characteristics such as words or syntax. Just as no single tree can represent the whole forest, he added, no individual text can represent an entire body of language. In his view, texts with definable boundaries (e.g., a complete conversation) are an ideal unit of observation in corpus research because they preserve explanatory information, such as the purpose and function of the text. He described these texts as fundamental units of discourse that constitute meaningful and valid social constructs and have integrity as a unit both situationally and linguistically.[6,7]

Egbert further explained that he seeks meaningful levels of analysis that fall between the individual text level and the complete body of language he is analyzing to enable classifying texts in useful ways. Traditionally, he noted, researchers have examined text in terms of geography, gender, age, or race, for example. In his view, however, the most important variable for explaining variation in texts across speakers and writers is register. He explained that registers are varieties of language defined by the situations in which they are used.[8] "There is a functional link between the language that is used and the situation that it is used in," he asserted, adding that research, including his own, has indicated that register can often explain why people make the language choices they do.[9] Thus, his research focuses on understanding the functional reasons for the language choices people make (e.g., using more or fewer verbs or nouns). Evidence suggests, he observed, that differences in register are detectable from the discourse level down to the level of speech sounds.

Egbert has been involved with a research project examining Internet language, which traditionally does not have clear categories of registers.[10] To assign categories of registers to this vast body of linguistic data, he

---

[6] Egbert, J., and Biber, D. (2016). Do all roads lead to Rome?: Modeling register variation with factor analysis and discriminant analysis. *Corpus Linguistics and Linguistic Theory*. doi: https://doi.org/10.1515/cllt-2016-0016.

[7] Biber, D., and Conrad, S. (2009). *Register, Genre, and Style* (Cambridge Textbooks in Linguistics). Cambridge, UK: Cambridge University Press. doi:10.1017/CBO9780511814358.

[8] Biber, D., and Conrad, S. (2009). *Register, Genre, and Style* (Cambridge Textbooks in Linguistics). Cambridge, UK: Cambridge University Press. doi:10.1017/CBO9780511814358.

[9] Biber, D. (2012). Register as a predictor of linguistic variation. *Corpus Linguistics and Linguistic Theory*, 8(1), 9–37.

[10] Biber, D., and Egbert, J. (2016). Register variation on the searchable web: A multidimensional analysis. *Journal of English Linguistics*, 44(2), 95–137.

elaborated, the researcher can predefine and sample from categories of interest, such as Twitter texts or YouTube video comments. An alternative method of sampling Internet texts, he explained, is to gather a random sample of texts and assign the texts to register categories in a bottom-up fashion. Using the latter method, Egbert and his colleagues collected a random sample of 50,000 texts, consisting of approximately 50 million words, from Google searches. Next, nearly 1,000 MTurk raters with minimal training coded each text for situational features, such as how interactive the text was, who its audience was, and what its purpose was. The researchers found that these nonexpert raters were unable to code the texts into register categories reliably. That being said, these nonexpert raters were able to code the texts for their situational features, which could then be used to generate categories of registers. Using this method, Egbert explained, the researchers were able to identify 8 categories of registers and 33 subregisters. They also found that although 4 raters rated each text and achieved nearly 70 percent agreement on the 8 register categories, 3 of 4 raters agreed just over half of the time (51.4%) on 33 subregister categories.

According to Egbert, the results of this research indicate that by using a bottom-up approach to identify registers in Internet language, one can detect variation in language use in register and subregister categories (e.g., use of first-person pronouns). He elaborated on these findings by showing how blogs, which are considered to be a meaningful text type, incorporate many different situations and registers. He then presented five major categories of blogs (see Table 4-1). Personal blogs, he noted, often contain first-personal pronouns because the author is writing about his or her own personal experiences. He contrasted this with informational blogs, where the use of first-person pronouns decreases because the focus of the writing is no longer the author. However, he cautioned, blogs do not constitute a

TABLE 4-1 Examples of Blog Registers

	Personal Blog	Travel Blog	Religious Blog	Opinion Blog	Informational Blog
Purpose	Narrative	Narrative/ description	Opinion	Opinion	Description
Subject	Author's life	Travel	Religion	Author's stance	Topic to be explained
Audience	Friends/ family/ followers	Travelers	Religious adherents	Various	Students/ nonexperts

SOURCE: Presentation by Jesse Egbert at the workshop.

register in themselves, even though they are often analyzed as a meaningful category in computational linguistic research. He explained further that mode of language (or the spoken or written method of communication) could also be considered as a unit of analysis. Spoken texts include transcribed interviews or song lyrics, for example.

Egbert reiterated that he views register as an important "signal" amid the "noise" of online linguistic information, and asserted that its use improves the usefulness and accuracy of computer algorithms employed in examining texts. "I think that we need to keep the linguistics in computational linguistics," he said. "This is critical considering the rapid increase in computational power in terms of speed [without] a corresponding increase in the availability of sound linguistic theory," he concluded.

DISCUSSION

Following the panel presentations, Matsumoto moderated a discussion. The discussion addressed (1) levels of analysis, (2) limitations of public opinion polling for learning about culture, and (3) the role of prediction.

Levels of Analysis

A member of the Intelligence Community (IC) shared his response to the issue of multiple levels of analysis in practical terms. A key concern of intelligence analysts, he explained, is how to convey essential information to decision makers effectively in a way that is compelling and trust building. "The time of who we are trying to convey information to is limited enough that they are going to need to quickly trust whatever is happening with [the methodology]," he noted, asserting that the methods described during the panel presentations would likely raise questions about the reliability of the interpretations they had generated. He emphasized that the ability to communicate clearly is at least as important as the rigor of the methods and the accuracy of the information. Another workshop participant, a former member of the IC, underscored the importance of communicating to decision makers. She explained that analysts seek to be informed by social science but not to use it overtly in their presentation of findings to decision makers.

The IC member explained that analysts rarely are able to choose the unit of analysis for the particular problem at hand. However, he observed that the various methods discussed during the panel presentations afforded flexibility that could be used to address gaps in explanatory narratives, and that presenters had related how various methodologies might be useful in building confidence in conclusions reached by researchers and analysts. Egbert noted that in his work, he examines text in context, and that this text represents people and the choices they have made within an exchange. Without context, he argued, interpretations will be incomplete or inaccurate.

Sutherlin asserted that the rich data now available should be used to improve predictions. No longer should people use maps that broadly label groups, she argued, because this approach oversimplifies conditions in an area and impedes informed decision making. Instead, she suggested that units of analysis should be as fine-grained as possible and then aggregated, given that, like weather forecasts, models and predictions are improved with the use of more fine-grained data. She suggested further that methods are needed with which to understand cultural differences because there are significant, foundational differences in the ways people from different cultures relay information. Without these understandings, she argued, interpretations will be very distorted, particularly if misunderstandings are used to train computer algorithms or are aggregated.

Gelfand suggested that it is also important to understand differences among the cultures of academics, the IC, and policy makers. "I think we need to understand the culture of your community," she said, adding that bridges between communities are needed. She also has observed that the strategy of trying to tell stories quickly and take action as rapidly as possible has backfired in cultures outside of the United States. Finally, she suggested that rather than identifying which levels of analysis are best, it is more important to identify how principles from one level of analysis can help inform analyses on other levels.

Limitations of Public Opinion Polling for Learning about Culture

Workshop participants discussed the benefits and drawbacks of public opinion polling as a means of understanding populations or individual actors. The IC often uses this approach, explained a former IC member. Gelfand, Egbert, and Sutherlin all emphasized the importance of triangulation.

Gelfand explained that "I do not trust any of my research until I see it with another method." In addition, she observed, polling can be problematic in cultures other than the United States where there is less openness and trust in talking to people conducting surveys. She also noted another limitation of public opinion polls that she has observed in her research. In her work interviewing former members of ISIS, she has found that they are unwilling to explain why they joined ISIS, but framing the question around why other people joined made them more willing to respond. She noted that few surveys ask questions about these descriptive norms.

Egbert emphasized that sampling is an important consideration in polling. Many polls are not representative, he observed, and many poll results are misreported or omit important information, such as the margin of error.

Sutherlin added that polls often parse their findings by gender, race, or age, but usually not by meaningful groups or communities that may be more relevant to understanding behavior and informing decision making. Thus, she said, she works to relate survey data to meaningful units within a particular society, such as families, tribes, or castes. She also related her experience of learning from other cultures during times of disaster or crisis, when people share their views through unstructured polling on important issues they are facing.

Dan Kahan, Yale University, explained his concerns with relying heavily on public opinion polls for decision making. First, he said, the opinions they describe often are statistical artifacts because people have limited information or opinions on the topics of many polls. Therefore, the opinion data are not revealing true sentiments on the topic as much as being a product of being asked about the topic in a poll. He illustrated the point by noting that most members of the public have no opinion about genetically modified organisms and eat them regularly, yet they will express an opinion on the subject if asked in a poll. Second, Kahan observed that polls are generally not constructed to measure or create coherent models of factors that explain people's behavior. Therefore, he argued, reliance on public polling data to understand how and why people behave as they do can be misleading.

Egbert also suggested that members of the IC may be especially interested in understanding outliers and anomalies in the data they analyze. Although he acknowledged that identifying such cases is difficult because of the "noise" in the data, he stressed that identifying cases that stand out from the baseline norms (e.g., threatening people) is important, and the stakes are high for being accurate. Another participant suggested that it is also important to understand the context and factors in the environment that may improve the prediction or understanding of outlier cases rather than waiting for outlier cases to occur.

Despite these concerns about relying on public opinion polls to achieve some of the analysis goals of the IC, Susan Weller, University of Texas Medical Branch, observed that it is important to distinguish such polls from federal surveys, which can be very useful data sources. Citing an example in health care, she noted that the National Health and Nutrition Examination Survey is carefully developed, pilot tested, and useful. She argued that although surveys are considered "old technology," professional and federal surveys remain extremely important.

The Role of Prediction

Presenters and panelists also discussed the meaning and importance of prediction in social and behavioral research and in the IC. A participant from the IC explained that when decision makers in the IC are presented with information related to prediction, they need to know what to do with that information. In addition, he said, they need to know important caveats about how the information should and should not be used, which may include information about the sampling or about the inferences that can be drawn from the data. "It is really important to do everything that we can to make sure that we recognize that what we are conveying will be used in that context," he stressed. "That is the difference between an applied and a theoretical world," he added. Sutherlin noted that she often seeks to avoid using the term "prediction," instead preferring to use such terminology as "to infer" or "to anticipate possibilities."

WRAP-UP

Asked by Matsumoto to convey how the social science community could help the IC over the next decade, a participant from the IC explained that the most important advance would be establishing a two-way dialogue between the two communities, which would allow the social science community to better understand the practicalities facing the IC. Another participant observed that the IC has an important deliberative process for weighing the evidence and alternative explanations provided by analysts. He added that this process includes communicating across agencies about outlier cases. Issues related to outliers are regular considerations of analysts and the IC more broadly when contending with risk and uncertainty, he said. One participant said, "What is needed is continued communication where government brings the notion of what the applied world looks like and academia brings theoretical insights, tools, and techniques. We are able to have a conversation with candor so that we can each learn from that. That is what I would like to have or that is the mechanism by which I would like to work over the next 10 years from my perspective."

Jeffrey Johnson, chair of the workshop steering committee, described several ways the social science community might be more helpful to the national security community. First, he noted that the IC gathers many types of data from various sources. The challenge for the social science community, he said, is to consider how it can communicate the insights derived from the methods for learning about culture, language, and behavior described during the workshop and help the IC integrate these insights with the data it is collecting on its own, such as polling data, survey data, and text data.

Second, Johnson suggested that the social science community consider the IC's needs for prediction. Although many social scientists are uncomfortable with that term, he said, providing the IC with probabilities of potential outcomes may still be useful.

Third, Johnson suggested that the social science community should consider how it can help build the trust and confidence of the national security comunity and the IC in its methodologies.

Finally, Johnson underscored the importance of understanding the various contexts of individuals. He emphasized the value of drawing on the different methodologies across many social science disciplines for that understanding.

Appendix A

Statement of Task for the Decadal Survey of Social and Behavioral Sciences for Applications to National Security

The National Academies of Sciences, Engineering, and Medicine will carry out a decadal survey on the social and behavioral sciences (SBS) in areas relevant to national security in two integrated phases. The first phase, a national summit (workshop), was completed in fall 2016. The statement of task for the second phase, a consensus process, is below.

An ad hoc consensus committee, drawing on membership from the summit steering committee, will be appointed to conduct the decadal survey aimed at identifying opportunities that are poised to contribute significantly to the Intelligence Community's (IC's) analytic responsibilities. The study will identify opportunities throughout the social sciences (e.g., sociology, demography, political science, economics, and anthropology) and from behavioral sciences (e.g., psychology, cognition, and neuroscience) and will draw on discussions at the summit to frame its inquiry. Attention will also be paid to work in allied professional disciplines such as engineering, business, and law, and a full variety of cross-disciplinary, historical, case study, participant, and phronetic approaches.

The committee will work with Office of the Director of National Intelligence and security community members to understand government needs and expectations. The final report will be based on the committee's consideration of broad national security priorities; relevant capabilities of elements within the security community to support and apply SBS research findings; cost and technical readiness; likely growth of research programs; emerging SBS data, procedures, personnel, and other resources; and opportunities to leverage related research activities not directly supported by government. The committee will specify a range of relevant work that could be useful to the IC for their consideration in developing future research priorities.

The committee's primary tasks will be to:

1. Assess progress in addressing selected major social and behavioral scientific challenges that might prove useful to national security. Include discussion of approaches that are gaining strength and those that are losing strength.
2, Identify SBS opportunities that can be used to guide security community investment decisions and application efforts over the next 10 years.
3. Specify approaches to facilitate productive interchange between the security community and the external social science research community.
4. Reflect on the application of the decadal model to the SBSs and identify lessons learned (insights into how to approach and perform the decadal survey process) and promising practices (activities that could facilitate future decadal surveys in the SBSs and similar disciplines and maximize their ultimate utilities to sponsors and the scientific community).

Appendix B

Workshop Agenda

CHANGING SOCIOCULTURAL DYNAMICS AND IMPLICATIONS
FOR NATIONAL SECURITY:
A WORKSHOP

October 11, 2017

Keck Center
500 Fifth Street, NW
Washington, DC
Room 206

8:30 a.m.   Workshop Registration Opens

9:00 a.m.   Workshops Commence

9:00 a.m.   Welcome and Overview of Events (Webcast from room 201)
Sujeeta Bhatt, Study Director
Audience Information
Paul Sackett, University of Minnesota, SBS Decadal Survey Chair
Welcome
David Honey, Director of Science and Technology, ODNI, Study Sponsor
Sponsor Perspective and Context for Study and Workshops

9:30 a.m.   Workshop Welcome and Ethical Considerations for SBS Research in Support of National Security
Jeffrey Johnson, University of Florida, Workshop Steering Committee Chair, SBS Decadal Survey Committee Member
Joy Rohde, University of Michigan, SBS Decadal Survey Committee Member, Workshop Steering Committee Member
Ethical Considerations for Digital SBS Research in Support of National Security

9:45 a.m.   Linking Culture, Language, Behavior, and Data

This session will bring together experts involved in the measurement of culture with those engaged in the study of culture, language, and behavior using big data and natural language processing to explore ways for applying these theoretical advancements in big data contexts. There have been recent theoretical developments in the study and measurement of culture. These approaches provide for a better conceptualization and quantification of culture and their potential relationship to behavior, and they have been applied to research at relatively small scales involving mostly primary data collection (e.g., face-to-face interviews). Can these approaches be applied to address larger scale issues in the study of culture at the regional and societal levels involving big data and data mining?

Susan Weller, University of Texas Medical Branch, Session Moderator, Workshop Steering Committee Member

Dan Kahan, Yale University
What Does Cultural Cognition Imply for National Security Risk Perceptions? You Tell Me!
William Dressler, University of Alabama
Cultural Consonance and Health: An Overview with Special Reference to Measurement
Dhiraj Murthy, University of Texas at Austin
Small Data to Big Data—Coding and Culture with Social Media Data

10:45 a.m. BREAK

11:00 a.m. Linking Culture, Language, Behavior and Data Panel Discussion
Susan Weller, Moderator
U. S. Government Participant Reaction
  Speakers will engage in a lively discussion regarding larger scale data issues in the study of culture

11:45 a.m. LUNCH

12:45 p.m. Cultural, Linguistic, and Behavioral Research and the Triangulation of Data

Multiple-method (or triangulation) and multiple-site (replication) research designs are increasingly used across the behavioral and social sciences. Although triangulation facilitates the validation of data through cross verification from more multiple sources and can be used to minimize the effects of bias and deepen one's understanding and insights into the study results, a number of questions still remain. For example, in cultural, linguistic, and behavioral research, how many sources of data are necessary to trust a conclusion? How do common elements across different contexts improve or hinder triangulation of cultural, linguistic, or behavioral data? What are key challenges in triangulating data that spans a variety of cultures, languages, geographies, data types, and levels of analyses? Thinking ahead to the next 10 years, where might a moderate investment lead to significant improvements in analysis of data using triangulation from a cultural, linguistic, and behavioral perspective?

Mark Liberman, University of Pennsylvania, Session Moderator, Workshop Steering Committee Member

Joe Labianca, University of Kentucky
  Identifying Positive and Negative Ties in Social Networks Through Triangulated Data
David Broniatowski, George Washington University
  Surveys, Laboratory Experiments, and Social Media: Better Together
Philip Resnik, University of Maryland, College Park
  The (In)Ability to Triangulate in Data-Driven Healthcare Research

1:45 p.m. Cultural, Linguistic, and Behavioral Research and the Triangulation of Data Panel Discussion
Mark Liberman, Moderator
U. S. Government Participant Reaction
   Speakers will engage in a lively discussion regarding issues and insights to analysis through the triangulation of data.

2:30 p.m. BREAK

2:45 p.m. Cultural, Linguistic, and Behavioral Research and the Challenge of Multiple Levels of Analysis

Cultural, linguistic, and behavioral analysis can be done at many levels of analysis with a variety of tools. This panel explores from an intelligence perspective these issues: (1) What research has been done to date that crosses and integrates culture-related data across multiple levels, domains, and disciplines? (2) What are the key challenges in selecting a level of analysis, or simultaneously exploring multiple levels of analysis when analyzing a situation from a cultural, linguistic, or behavioral perspective? (3) How can you tell that the wrong level of analysis has been chosen and what are the potential policy ramifications? (4) How are or will new technologies for online data collection and processing impacting the way cultural, linguistic, and behavioral research is conducted at multiple levels? (5) Thinking ahead to the next 10 years, where might a moderate investment lead to significant improvements in multi-level analysis from a cultural, linguistic, and behavioral perspective?

David Matsumoto, San Francisco State University; Session Moderator, SBS Decadal Survey Committee Member, Workshop Steering Committee Member

Gwyneth Sutherlin, Geographic Services, Inc.
   Levels of Influence
Michele Gelfand, University of Maryland, College Park
   Tightness-Looseness: A Fractal Pattern of Cultural Variation
Jesse A. Egbert, Northern Arizona University
   Meaningful Levels of Analysis in (corpus) Linguistics

3:45 p.m.   Cultural, Linguistic, and Behavioral Research and the Challenge of Multiple Levels of Analysis Panel Discussion
David Matsumoto, Moderator
U. S. Government Participant Reaction
 Speakers will engage in a lively discussion regarding issues concerning levels of analysis in all disciplines, and how to overcome them in order to generate more integrated, cohesive views of culture and behavior.

4:30 p.m.   Roundtable Discussion of Presentations and Wrap-Up
Jeffrey Johnson, SBS Decadal Survey Committee Member, Workshop Steering Committee Member

5:00 p.m.   ADJOURN

Appendix C

Participants List

Listed here are the individuals who attended one or more of three workshops held October 11, 2017, to gather information for the Decadal Survey of Social and Behavioral Sciences for Applications to National Security.

Vincent Alcazar
Vincent Alcazar, LLC

Alexandra Beatty
National Academies

Andrew Bennett
Georgetown University

Gary G. Berntson
The Ohio State University

Sujeeta Bhatt
National Academies

Jordan A. Blenner
Lewis-Burke Associates, LLC

Matthew Brashears
University of South Carolina

Christa Brelsford
Oak Ridge National Laboratory

David Broniatowski
George Washington University

Dennis Buede
Innovative Decisions, Inc.

Rita Bush
National Security Agency

Kathleen Carley
Carnegie Mellon University

Lina Cepeda
United Nations

Guido Cervone
Pennsylvania State University

Hsinchun Chen
University of Arizona

Richard Cincotta
Stimson Center

Kyle Clark
U.S. Department of Homeland Security

Noshir Contractor
Northwestern University

Bradley Cooke
National Science Foundation, AAAS S&T Policy Fellow

Chris Cox
Defense Intelligence Agency

Thelma Cox
National Academies

Skyler Cranmer
Ohio State University

Bruce Crawford
Independent Researcher

Leslie DeChurch
Northwestern University

Daniel Demus
Defense Threat Reduction Agency

David Dornisch
U.S. Government Accountability Office

Barbara Anne Dosher
University of California, Irvine

Jennifer Dresden
Georgetown University

William Dressler
University of Alabama

Anna Duran
Avatar Research Institute

Jesse A. Egbert
Northern Arizona University

Kacey Ernst
University of Arizona

Emily Falk
University of Pennsylvania

Scott Feld
Purdue University

Suzanne Fry
National Intelligence Council

George G.
U.S. Government

Sumit Ganguly
Indiana University

Michele Gelfand
University of Maryland

Christopher Gelpi
The Ohio State University

James Goldgeier
American University

Benjamin Golub
Harvard University

Hal Greenwald
MITRE

Richard Harknett
University of Cincinnati

Winston Harris
Defense Threat Reduction Agency

Jesse Hoey
University of Waterloo

Michael Holtje
U.S. Department of Treasury

David Honey
Office of the Director of National Intelligence

John Hoven
Independent Consultant

Judith Jacobson
Innovative Decisions, Inc.

Gary Jin
U.S. Department of Homeland Security

Jeffrey C. Johnson
University of Florida

Kenny Joseph
Northeastern University

Regina Joseph
New York University

Dan Kahan
Yale University

Sallie Keller
Virginia Polytechnic Institute and State University

Jacklyn Kerr
Stanford University

Giuseppe (Joe) Labianca
University of Kentucky

Deborah Larson
University of California, Los Angeles

Mark Liberman
University of Pennsylvania

Herb Lin
Stanford University

Sean Lynn-Jones
Harvard University

Anthony Mann
National Academies

David Matsumoto
San Francisco State University

Shana McLean
IARPA

Carmen Medina
MedinAnalytics, LLC

Asma Melebrai
Government Contractor

Katherine Meyer
National Science Foundation

Marc Dean Millot
Good Harbor Partners

Mahmoud Moamenah
Government Contractor

Markus Mobius
Microsoft Research

Fran P. Moore
FPM Consulting, LLC

Amanda Murdie
University of Georgia

Dhiraj Murthy
University of Texas

Kent Myers
Office of the Director of National Intelligence

Zachary Neal
Michigan State University

Howard C. Nusbaum
National Science Foundation

Robert O'Connor
National Science Foundation

Nedim Ogelman
U.S. State Department

Carolyn Parkinson
University of California, Los Angeles

Randolph H. Pherson
Pherson Associates, LLC

Jennarose Placitella
University of Pennsylvania

Ted Plasse
U.S. Department of Defense

Alyson Reed
Linguistic Society of America

Philip Resnik
University of Maryland

Joy Rohde
University of Michigan

Benjamin Ryan
Gallup, Inc.

Paul R. Sackett
University of Minnesota

Laura Sappelsa
ANSER

Julie Schuck
National Academies

Afreen Siddiqi
Massachusetts Institute of Technology

Michael Siri
National Academies

Robert Smith
University of Maryland

Laura Steckman
MITRE

Anita Street
Office of the Director of National Intelligence

Jim Sullivan
Central Intelligence Agency

Gwyneth Sutherlin
Geographic Services, Inc.

Jeffrey Taliaferro
Tufts University

Steve Thompson
Office of the Director of National
    Intelligence

William R. Thompson
Indiana University

Elizabeth Townsend
National Academies

Lisa Troyer
Army Research Office

Garrett Tyson
National Academies

Stuart Umpleby
George Washington University

Alexander Volfovsky
Duke University

Kate Von Holle
University of Chicago

Barbara Wanchisen
National Academies

Steven Ward
Cornell University

Susan Weller
University of Texas

Mitzi Wertheim
Naval Postgraduate School

Renée L. Wilson Gaines
National Academies

Jeremy Wolfe
Brigham and Women's Hospital,
    Harvard Medical School

Mary Zalesny
Defense Threat Reduction Agency

Appendix D

Biographical Sketches of Steering Committee Members and Presenters

Sujeeta Bhatt (*Study Director*) is a senior program officer with the National Academies of Sciences, Engineering, and Medicine and study director for the Decadal Survey of Social and Behavioral Sciences for Applications to National Security. She was formerly a research scientist at the Defense Intelligence Agency (DIA) and was detailed to the Federal Bureau of Investigation's High-Value Detainee Interrogation Group (HIG). Prior to that, she was an assistant professor in the Department of Radiology at the Georgetown University Medical Center on detail to DIA/HIG. Her work at DIA and HIG entailed identifying knowledge gaps and developing and managing research projects to address those gaps. Her work in the Intelligence Community focused on the psychological and neuroscience bases for credibility assessment, biometrics, insider threat, intelligence interviewing and interrogation methods, and the development of research-to-practice modules on interrogation-related topics to promote the use of evidence-based practice in interviews/interrogations. Dr. Bhatt holds a Ph.D. in behavioral neuroscience from American University.

David Broniatowski (*Presenter*) is an assistant professor in the School of Engineering and Applied Science at George Washington University and director of the Decision Making and Systems Architecture Laboratory. He conducts research on decision making under risk, group decision making, system architecture, and behavioral epidemiology. This research program draws on a wide range of techniques, including formal mathematical modeling, experimental design, automated text analysis and natural language processing, social and technical network analysis, and big data. Current projects include a text network analysis of transcripts from meetings of the U.S. Food and Drug Administration's Circulatory Systems Advisory Panel, a mathematical formalization of fuzzy trace theory, and a study using Twitter data to conduct surveillance of influenza infection and the resulting social response. Dr. Broniatowski received a Ph.D. in engineering systems from the Massachusetts Institute of Technology.

Kathleen Carley (*Committee Member*) is a professor of computer science in the Institute for Software Research and director of the Center for Computational Analysis of Social and Organizational Systems at Carnegie Mellon University. She is also CEO of Carley Technologies Inc., also known as Netanomics. Her research combines cognitive science, sociology, and computer science to address complex social and organizational issues. Her most notable research contribution was the establishment of dynamic network analysis (DNA) and the associated theory and methodology for examining large high-dimensional time-variant networks. Her research on DNA has resulted in tools for analyzing and visualizing large-scale dynamic networks and various multiagent simulation systems. She is the developer of a high-dimensional network analysis and visualization system, ORA, that supports network analytics in general, for social media, and for dynamic and geospatial networks. Her group has also developed tools for extracting sentiment, social, and semantic networks from social media and other textual data (AutoMap); simulating epidemiological models (BioWar); simulating covert networks (DyNet); and simulating changes in beliefs and practice given information campaigns (Construct). She is a fellow of the Institute of Electrical and Electronics Engineers. Dr. Carley holds a Ph.D. in sociology from Harvard University.

William Dressler (*Presenter*) is a professor of anthropology at the University of Alabama. His research examines the relationship between culture and health, including concepts and methods for examining the health effects of individual efforts to achieve culturally defined goals and aspirations in settings as diverse as urban Great Britain, the southeastern United States, the West Indies, Mexico, and Brazil. Over the past 30 years, Dr. Dressler and his Brazilian colleagues have carried out four major projects on health in Brazil showing that difficulties in achieving culturally defined goals in Brazilian society are associated with increased risk of high blood pressure, obesity, depression, and poor immune function. Dr. Dressler also has served on the faculties of the University of Alabama School of Medicine–Tuscaloosa and the School of Social Work. He received a Ph.D. in anthropology from the University of Connecticut.

Jesse Egbert (*Presenter*) is an assistant professor of applied linguistics at Northern Arizona University. He specializes in the use of corpus linguistic methods to explore patterns of language variation across registers, particularly academic prose and the Internet. His research also explores issues related to quantitative linguistic research, including corpus design and representativeness, methodological triangulation, and the application of advanced statistical techniques to language data. Dr. Egbert has received a number of academic awards and research grants and holds a Ph.D. in applied linguistics from Northern Arizona University.

Michele Gelfand (*Presenter*) is a distinguished university professor in the Department of Psychology at the University of Maryland, College Park. Her research interests include cross-cultural social and organizational behavior; cultural influences on conflict, negotiation, justice, revenge, and forgiveness; discrimination and sexual harassment; and theory and method in assessing aspects of culture (individualism–collectivism, cultural tightness–looseness). She has conducted research across many cultures, using field, experimental, computational, and neuroscientific methods to understand the evolution of cultural differences and their consequences for individuals, teams, organizations, and nations. She has also done work on the role of culture in negotiation and conflict and the psychology of revenge and forgiveness. She is the recipient of several awards and editor of a number of books and series. She was president of the International Association for Conflict Management from 2009 to 2010. She holds both an M.A. and a Ph.D. in social/organizational psychology from the University of Illinois, Urbana–Champaign.

David A. Honey (*Sponsor*) serves as director of science and technology and as assistant deputy director of national intelligence for science and technology in the Office of the Director of National Intelligence. He is responsible for the development of effective strategies, policies, and programs that lead to the successful integration of science and technology capabilities into operational systems. Prior to this assignment, he served as deputy assistant secretary of defense, research, in the Office of the Assistant Secretary of Defense. He was director of the Defense Advanced Research Projects Agency's Strategic Technology Office, director of the Advanced Technology Office, and deputy director and program manager of the Microsystems Technology Office. He is a retired Air Force lieutenant colonel who began his military career as a pilot. He received a Ph.D. in solid state science from Syracuse University.

Jeffrey Johnson (*Committee Chair*) is a professor of anthropology at the University of Florida. He is also an adjunct professor in the Institute for

Software Research at Carnegie Mellon University. He was director of the Summer Institute for Research Design in Cultural Anthropology from 1996 to 2015. He was also a program manager with the Army Research Office (Intergovernmental Personnel Act), where he started the basic science research program in the social sciences. He has conducted extensive long-term research comparing group dynamics and the evolution of social networks of overwintering crews at the American South Pole Station and at the Polish, Russian, Chinese, and Indian Antarctic Stations. Using these isolated human group settings as space analogs, he is currently studying the role of aspects of team cognition in mission success. He received a Ph.D. in social science from the University of California, Irvine.

Dan Kahan (*Presenter*) is Elizabeth K. Dollard professor of law and a professor of psychology at Yale Law School. He is a member of the Cultural Cognition Project, an interdisciplinary team of scholars who use empirical methods to examine the impact of group values on perceptions of risk and science communication. In studies funded by the National Science Foundation, he and his collaborators have investigated public dissensus over climate change, public reactions to emerging technologies, and public understandings of scientific consensus across disputed issues. The project's current focus is on field research aimed at integrating insights from the science of science communication into the craft of professional science communicators in various domains, including democratic decision making, education, and popular engagement with science. Professor Kahan is a senior fellow at the National Center for Science and Civic Engagement and a member of the American Academy of Arts and Sciences. He holds a J.D. from Harvard Law School.

Giuseppe (Joe) Labianca (*Presenter*) is Gatton chaired professor of management and co-director of the LINKS Social Network Analysis Center in the Gatton College of Business and Economics, University of Kentucky. His main research interest is understanding interpersonal conflict from a social network perspective, including understanding how dyads in conflict within an organization are affected by third parties. He also conducts research on the social networks of groups, as well as on how individuals' cognitions about organizational change and justice are affected by their network ties. Prior to joining the Gatton School, he was on the faculty of the Goizueta Business School at Emory University and the Freeman School of Business at Tulane University, and served as a research fellow at Pennsylvania State University's Center for Research on Conflict and Negotiation. He received a Ph.D. in business administration from Pennsylvania State University.

Mark Liberman *(Committee Member)* is director of the Linguistics Data Consortium, faculty director of the Ware College House, Christopher H. Browne distinguished professor of linguistics in the Department of Linguistics, and professor in the Department of Computer and Information Science at the University of Pennsylvania. His research focuses on corpus-based phonetics; speech and language technology; the phonology and phonetics of lexical tone and its relationship to intonation; gestural, prosodic, morphological, and syntactic ways of marking focus and their use in discourse; formal models for linguistic annotation; information retrieval and information extraction from text; the organization of spoken communication in the human brain, especially in relation to the evolutionary substrates for speech and language and to analogous systems in other animals; and agent-based models of language evolution and learning. His early research established the linguistic subfield of metrical phonology. Much of his current research is conducted through computational analyses of linguistic corpora. He is the recipient of several awards in the field of linguistics. He received his M.S. and Ph.D. in linguistics from the Massachusetts Institute of Technology.

David Matsumoto *(Committee Member)* is a professor of social psychology at San Francisco State University and director of the Culture and Emotion Research Lab, which focuses on studies involving culture, emotion, social interaction, and communication. He is well known for his work in the field of microexpressions, facial expression, gesture, and nonverbal behavior. He holds a Ph.D. in psychology from the University of California, Berkeley.

Dhiraj Murthy *(Presenter)* is an associate professor of journalism and sociology at the University of Texas at Austin. Prior to his academic career, he was a network engineer and UNIX systems administrator. His work explores social media, digital research methods, race/ethnicity, qualitative/mixed methods, big data quantitative analysis, and virtual organizations. He is currently funded by the National Science Foundation's Division of Computer and Network Systems for pioneering work on the use of social media during Hurricane Harvey. In this project, he is developing coding ontologies derived from qualitative fieldwork that can be applied to big data environments. Dr. Murthy founded and directs the Computational Media Lab at the University of Texas at Austin. He received a Ph.D. in sociology from the University of Cambridge.

Philip Resnik *(Presenter)* is director of the University of Maryland Computational Linguistics and Information Processing Laboratory. He holds joint appointments in the Department of Linguistics and at the University of Maryland Institute for Advanced Computer Studies and is an affiliate professor in the Department of Computer Science. His research focuses on computational social science and computational psycholinguistics. His interests include the application of natural language processing techniques to such practical problems as machine translation and sentiment analysis, computational models in social science, and the modeling of human linguistic processes (especially related to lexical semantics). Dr. Resnik's general research agenda for language technology is to improve the state of the art by finding the right balance between data-driven statistical modeling and the use of linguistic and expert domain knowledge, with the larger goal of obtaining a better scientific understanding of human language itself. He holds a Ph.D. in computer and information science from the University of Pennsylvania.

Joy Rohde (*Committee Member*) is an assistant professor at the Gerald R. Ford School of Public Policy, University of Michigan. She is also a faculty member with the Science, Technology, and Society Program and the Department of History. Her work examines the relationship between the social and behavioral sciences and the American state from the late 19th century to the present. She is currently working on a book project that explores how ideas about cybernetics and advances in computing have impacted the social sciences, policy analysis, and national security in the United States since the 1960s. Prior to joining the Ford School, Dr. Rohde was an assistant professor of history at Trinity University, and she has held fellowships from the Miller Center of Public Affairs and the American Academy of Arts and Sciences. She received a Ph.D. in history and sociology of science from the University of Pennsylvania.

Paul Sackett (*Decadal Survey Chair*) is Beverly and Richard Fink distinguished professor of psychology and liberal arts at the University of Minnesota. His research interests revolve around various aspects of testing and assessment in workplace, educational, and military settings. He has served as president of the Society for Industrial and Organizational Psychology, as co-chair of the committee producing the Standards for Educational and Psychological Testing, as a member of the National Research Council's Board on Testing and Assessment, as chair of the American Psychological Association's (APA's) Committee on Psychological Tests and Assessments, and as chair of APA's Board of Scientific Affairs. He holds a Ph.D. in industrial/organizational psychology from Ohio State University.

Gwyneth Sutherlin (*Presenter*) is director of human geography and analytics research at Geographic Services, Inc. As a researcher, she focuses on the intersection of cultural dimensions and technology for application in conflict analysis, with insights stemming from cognitive linguistics, cultural dynamics, and empirical study. In the field, her work on multilingual communications in conflict environments has included designing a program to impact identity narratives through media in North Africa that garnered United Nations recognition for innovation. Her research seeking to bridge social science and engineering has included an analysis of crowdsourcing data for decision making in Haiti, Somalia, and the Arab Spring and integration of cultural variables in open-source communication models supporting policy decisions. She operates in seven foreign languages. Currently, her research in human geography supports various U.S. government agencies and international nongovernmental organizations with analysis, including contributions to the Strategic Multilayer Assessment group out of the Joint Staff J39. Dr. Sutherlin holds a Ph.D. in peace and conflict studies from the University of Bradford.

Susan Weller (*Committee Member*) is a professor in the Division of Sociomedical Sciences in the Department of Preventive Medicine and Community Health and director of the research program in the Department of Family Medicine at the University of Texas Medical Branch. She is recognized nationally and internationally for her expertise in the area of research methods and is skilled in both qualitative and quantitative methods. Her research interests span topics in both medicine (diabetes, AIDS, and asthma) and the social sciences (social support, stress, and folk illnesses). Dr. Weller is co-developer of the Cultural Consensus Model, a mathematical method for estimating cultural beliefs. She has served on a number of expert scientific advisory committees and boards, including a consensus panel to summarize research concerning condoms and sexually transmitted diseases. She received a B.A. and Ph.D. in social science from the University of California, Irvine.